GREAT WRITERS AS INTERPRETERS
OF RELIGION

GREAT WRITERS AS INTERPRETERS OF RELIGION

By

EDWIN MIMS

Professor Emeritus of English Literature
Vanderbilt University

ABINGDON-COKESBURY PRESS

New York • *Nashville*

GREAT WRITERS AS INTERPRETERS OF RELIGION
COPYRIGHT, MCMXLV
BY WHITMORE & STONE

K

Printed in the United States of America

25-403

TO THE MEMORY OF
MY SON

Edwin Mims, Jr.

PREFACE

THE invitation of Dean John K. Benton and the faculty of the School of Religion of Vanderbilt University to deliver one of two series of lectures in celebration of the fiftieth anniversary of the Cole Lectureship Foundation was easy for me to accept. It afforded an opportunity to formulate and crystallize what had been the burden of my teaching for fifty years, namely, the magnifying of the spiritual values and the religious elements in English and American literature. The response of the Vanderbilt community and the people of Nashville suggested that I might, on the basis of these lectures, extend the treatment and offer the result to a larger public.

While these chapters were being prepared and rewritten in a less academic style, I had the opportunity as a national lecturer for Phi Beta Kappa and as a representative of the Association of American Colleges to talk to college communities in all parts of the country, emphasizing that religion and literature should be stressed in any program of liberal education. Meanwhile Dr. William K. Anderson, secretary of the Commission on Ministerial Training of the Methodist Church, provided me opportunity to talk to schools and institutes of preachers on the importance of literature in any program of religious education. The response of these various audiences has caused me to hope that this volume may appeal to a rather wide circle of those interested in literature and in religion.

Readers of this book may feel that the last chapter is an

inadequate treatment of the exposition in literature of Jesus as the central fact in Christian faith. Poets other than Browning have interpreted the Christ. Within a few weeks of the Cole lectures referred to above I delivered a series of Shaffer lectures at Northwestern University on the subject "Jesus in English and American Poetry," in which was developed more fully the point of view of the last chapter of this volume. An expansion of the Shaffer lectures is being prepared for later publication.

I wish to acknowledge my indebtedness to Dean Benton for his sympathetic co-operation in the preparation of the Cole lectures and in the further extension of the plan to reach a larger audience. I have made use, in assembling some of the material, of articles that appeared originally in *The Methodist Review* and *The Southern Methodist Quarterly Review*. I am grateful to Charles Scribner's Sons for allowing me to adapt parts of the introduction to my edition of Carlyle's *Past and Present*. Acknowledgments of quotations from copyrighted material are made in the places where the quotations occur.

EDWIN MIMS

CONTENTS

LITERATURE AS A PERSONAL RESOURCE

To GIVE expression to what we see and hear, feel and experience, is one of our primary needs. It may be said with emphasis that no one has had an emotion or idea until he has found expression for it—an expression that is at once "adequate, felicitious, and final." Most of us have to say with Tennyson,

> And I would that my tongue could utter
> The thoughts that arise in me.

And we are so much the more happy when a choice quotation seems, in the words of Pope, "what oft was thought, but ne'er so well expressed."

Literature, and especially poetry, is pre-eminently the art of expression. It is not a question of *what* is said but of *how*. We may all have something of the same idea, but the expression of that idea may be merely conventional, stereotyped, abstract, or it may be concrete, artistic, consummate. A good illustration is Kipling's "Recessional," written at the end of the celebration of Queen Victoria's Diamond Jubilee. Everyone felt that the word for which he had waited had been spoken, and it has continued to be a great hymn. Likewise, Wordsworth's "Character of the Happy Warrior" comes inevitably to one who is trying to phrase

11

the characteristics of any typical hero of the English-speaking people.

The responsibility of finding proper expression, either by our own original way of looking at things or by knowing where we can find the best expression, is therefore very great. The art of interpretation is as essential as conviction or faith. The most terrible indictment ever brought against ministers and teachers is Milton's line in "Lycidas," "The hungry sheep look up, and are not fed"—unless we except the words of John Donne, "The infirmity of the preacher diminisheth the Word." Think of what is involved in those two sentences: the shepherd leading his flock, not into green pastures or beside still waters, but into desert sands and the rocky hardness of the wilderness; God's interpreter, by his infirmity of expression, actually diminishing the word that ought to come burning from his lips. Yes, the word must become flesh before it can move the minds and hearts of men. As George Herbert, at once poet and saint, said, "A verse may find him who a sermon flies." Literature in a very real sense is the word made flesh, and fortunate is the man who has at his command "the record of the happiest and best moments of the best and happiest men."

This power and charm of expression has been applied in our heritage of literature to every phase of human life and thought, to every emotion, every idea, to every type of personality. For the creative writer does not invent a world out of space and out of time; he finds his material in the world about him, and it is his genius to give notable expression to all he finds. Most of us have eyes and see not, ears and hear not, until some man of imagination unseals our eyes and unstops our ears. As Browning's Fra Lippo Lippi says,

12

> We're made so that we love
> First when we see them painted, things we have passed
> Perhaps a hundred times nor cared to see.

So literature teaches us what we could have known but for our limitations of blindness and deafness, but it goes further and enables us to transcend our limitations of time, of place, and of personality. If we cannot become heirs of all the ages, we may at least come into the inheritance of those periods of history which find expression in literature, for it cannot be emphasized too strongly that every age has been crystallized in its literature. If we cannot become citizens of the world, we may live in imagination in those places which have been revealed and interpreted by great writers. If we cannot be other than ourselves or know truly more than a few personalities among family and close friends, we can yet enter into the personalities of writers and of characters created by them; and every personality that we comprehend is an addition to our personality. As we overcome all these limitations, we

> may rise on stepping-stones
> Of [our] dead selves to higher things.

This is the secret of never growing old. Perpetual youth may be found in reading the great writings which, in the phrase of Emerson,

> find us young,
> And always keep us so.

Surely, then, it ought not to be necessary to emphasize the contemporary value of great classics. Those who believe

13

that the Bible is as much alive today as when its various books were written or translated ought not to believe that because something was written one hundred years ago or even one thousand or more years ago it is dead stuff. There is a great danger that even the best of us may be too much influenced by the constant pressure to read the new books that come so thick and fast from our publishing houses. The Book-of-the-Month Club, yes, even the Religious Book-of-the-Month Club, the tempting lists of best-sellers, the alluring blurbs or jackets seen in bookstores everywhere, the facile and conscienceless reviews in periodicals that are too much influenced by advertising managers—all these tend to lead us away from the books that have upon them the stamp of the ages, that we know to be good and valuable for men of all time. After all, art is timeless; nature is always as young as "when first God dawned on Chaos"; human nature is always pretty much the same even though it manifests itself in various forms. There are just a few universal themes; and these, expressed by creative artists of many generations, "age cannot wither . . . nor custom stale." As a distinguished educator said not long ago, "We have listened too much to the dead voices of the living, and not enough to the living voices of the dead."

II

Of literature as the expression of great thoughts and of the contemporary value of writings from other ages there is no better illustration than the speeches of Winston Churchill in this great crisis of world history. A master of expression himself, both as a historian and as an orator, he often in his perorations uses a passage of poetry to clinch and make effective his ideas—for instance, his dramatic use of Longfellow's often-quoted passage on the Ship of State, Arthur Hugh Clough's "Say not the struggle nought availeth," and passages from Kipling and Walt Whitman.

He is in line with the tradition of English statesmen, many of whom have been men of letters as well as masters of political science and great administrators. Woodrow Wilson once wrote an essay on "Mere Literature" in which he pleads for the study of English literature as an essential in all education. Read carefully, it has its meaning for leaders who stand for high ideals in individual and national life:

[Literature] opens our hearts to receive the experiences of great men and the conceptions of great races. . . . It airs our souls in the wide atmosphere of contemplation. . . . If this free people to which we belong is to keep its fine spirit, its perfect temper amidst affairs, its high courage in the face of difficulties, its wise temperateness and wide-eyed hope, it must continue to drink deep and often from the old wells of English undefiled, quaff the keen tonic of its best ideals, keep its blood warm with the great utterances of exalted purpose and pure principles of which its matchless literature is full. The great spirits of the past must command us to the tasks of the future.

There could be no better evidence that literature does not belong to specialists, but is the common inheritance of all "who speak the tongue that Shakespeare spake." Thomas Henry Huxley was the foremost leader in the popularization of scientific knowledge and in the establishment of the natural sciences in our educational program, but where will one find a stronger statement of the need for the study of English literature than in his essay on "Science and Culture"? One of our very best institutions for the training of engineers, chemists, and physicists is the California Institute of Technology; and yet the men who have been most responsible for its success—Millikan, Noyes, and Hale—are all men of wide culture, who saw the necessity of requiring the humane studies in all four years of the curriculum. The Hall of the Humanities is one of the central buildings on the campus. Furthermore, an increasing number of business executives in all parts of the country are insisting that they prefer men who have been trained in liberal arts colleges rather than in strictly technical schools.

Charles A. Beard, who wrote the *Charter for the Social Sciences in the Schools,* the very best statement of the need for such studies, has recently summarized the need for supplementing economics and sociology by increased attention to ethics and aesthetic values. No longer can they be regarded as irrelevant or incidental in education. "At its very center is knowledge of good and beautiful things, and conduct which has been brought to realization, if only here and there, and in fragmentary form; around this knowledge the imagination of the artist and ethical thinker creates new goods and beauties which effort can bring into being."

Many other illustrations might be cited to show the place of literature in the lives of men of all professions. Sir William Osler, who was the greatest physician in the English-speaking world in his generation, and who influenced medical education more than any other man, spent the last half hour of every day reading his beloved classics, and wrote essays that in their charm of literary allusions rank with the best of our time. The late Justice Holmes found time in his very busy life as a lawyer and judge to read widely in philosophy and literature. John Richard Green contended that English literature is the very soul of the life and thought of the English people. John Morley, historian, biographer, and

16

statesman, said that "the greatest need in modern culture, which is scientific in method, rationalistic in spirit, and utilitarian in purpose, is to find some effective method for cherishing within us the ideal," and that literature is the greatest single agency for that end. Many have found that reading in economics and sociology is vitalized when they know Ruskin and Carlyle, modern novelists and dramatists, or poems like "The Man with the Hoe."

Philosophers have found in literature one of the best aids to creative thinking. For, aside from its appeal to the emotions, literature is the highest form of inspired intuition, or the total man thinking in terms of the imagination. That is why Coleridge said that there was never a great poet who was not a philosopher—not that he passed through the processes of philosophical thought, but that he arrived at his conclusions by a leap of the prepared imagination. How much richer in subject matter and in expression is William James than many of our modern psychologists; and all because he had at his command a wide range of English and world literature. Santayana summed up what he considered the three main philosophies in his study of Lucretius (materialism), Dante (supernaturalism), and Goethe (humanism). The reader of Josiah Royce's *The Spirit of Modern Philosophy* is impressed with the fact that at the conclusion of his discussion of each philosopher he invariably calls to his aid some passage of poetry or imaginative prose. Whitehead, the latest of the great philosophers, in his *Science and the Modern World* criticizes science as limited in its outlook because it abstracts from real objects only those qualities which may be scientifically known: "One may know all about the sun and the laws of light and the rotation of the earth and yet miss the radiance of the sunset."

17

Hence his emphasis on the aesthetic appreciation of the universe, and his frequent use of Wordsworth, Tennyson, and Shelley to reinforce his idea of wonder and mystery.

III

It is no wonder, then, that like the great minds in other fields the leaders of religious thought have found literature a constant influence and inspiration, a source of comfort and courage, and often an interpretation of the fundamental Christian virtues. One cannot read John Wesley's diary, or a biography of Martin Luther, one cannot have heard the great preachers of our time without realizing that literature is one of the means by which God has inspired the revelation and expression of truth. Archdeacon Farrar made a sweeping statement when he wrote:

I dare to say that I have learned more of high and holy teaching from Dante and Shakespeare, Milton and Wordsworth, Browning and Tennyson, than I have learned from many of the professed divines. The poets have given me more consolation in sorrow, more passion for righteousness, more faith in the divine goodness, more courage to strive after the attainment of the divine ideal, more insight into the sacred charities which save us from despairing over the littleness of man, than I have derived from other men. . . . Next to [the prophets and apostles of the Bible], of all human teachers, I should place the illumined souls of the few Christian poets of the world who, sweeping aside the sham and rubbish of pharisaism, lead us to realities and to the living Christ.

Some of our greatest recent and contemporary preachers —for example, John Kelman, S. Parkes Cadman, Bishop Francis J. McConnell, Charles W. Gilkey, and Lynn Harold

Hough—would endorse that statement. Indeed many such prophets of God might well be called teachers of literature, so closely related in their minds are genuine literary culture and vital religion. I recall that the late Dean Wilbur F. Tillett, who trained many a notable preacher of our day, gave for years in the School of Religion of Vanderbilt University a course on the religious teachings of the poets along with his course on systematic theology, the one supplementing the other. Dr. Harry Emerson Fosdick, in his recently published *On Being a Real Person*, states strongly the necessity for finding in literature one of the chief aids to religion:

More frequently I have turned to biography and autobiography, and to those novelists, poets, and dramatists who have been, as was said of of Shakespeare, circumnavigators of the human soul. Indeed, I have done this so much that I fear some casual reader's misapprehension about the multiplied allusions and quotations with which this book is filled. If one thinks of them as intended to be decorative, or even in a popular sense illustrative, my purpose in using them is completely misunderstood. They are intended to be case studies and so a substantial part of the argument. Nowhere are the common frustrating experiences of personal life more vividly described, our familiar mental and emotional maladjustments more convincingly portrayed, than in biographies and autobiographies, poems, novels, and dramas, and this rich storehouse of psychological self-revelation and insight has been too much neglected.[1]

In other words, a doctor of souls finds literature a sovereign medicine. So too in his widely read book *Prayer* Dr. George A. Buttrick quotes from or alludes to more than

[1] By permission of the publisher, Harper & Bros.

fifty great writers, finding in them veritable manuals of devotion and piety. And the great English preacher Dr. Leslie D. Weatherhead in a profound study of the poets of the nineteenth century discovered abundant material for an inspiring book on immortality, *The Afterworld of the Poets*.

IV

Almost every day the English weather bureau issues a forecast something like this: "Rain, showers, fog, mist, disagreeable weather, bright intervals." Anybody who has ever traveled in England realizes what those bright intervals mean. The phrase is symbolic of life at its best. A Frenchman once said: "When you are turning a grindstone, every moment counts the same; but when you are doing a great work, the inspired moments are precious." Life is a matter of dull routine unless there are such moments to add glory and significance to its value. The right use of one's leisure becomes a matter of profound importance. The enjoyment of music, the appreciation of beauty in nature and in art, communion with the Eternal, are all necessary to fit us for any emergency that may arise, for any disappointment or disillusionment; but none of these surpass the greatest literature in the enrichment of life.

CHAPTER I

HARMONIZERS OF CULTURE AND RELIGION

ALL would agree that the reading or study of literature is one of the indispensable elements in culture, but some would ask what it has to do with religion. In many minds there is a conflict between culture and religion. Rightly understood, the two are not opposites but are identical, or at least complementary.

Sixty odd years ago James Thomson, the author of *The City of Dreadful Night,* in a paper read before the Browning Society of London suggested the subject "How Can Browning Be a Christian?" He could not understand how a man with such varied interests and attainments, a man who was at home in the fields of music, art, science, literature, and social life, could be a Christian—a term that to Thomson indicated a narrow outlook on life and was associated with medieval asceticism and Puritanism. Without attempting to answer that question now, I cite it as an illustration of the attitude of a good many people—highly cultivated people—to religion.

Phillips Brooks, in his childhood dedicated to the ministry by a pious mother and by his own will, was so impressed during his years at Harvard by what has since been called "the flowering of New England" that he came to feel he could not confine himself within the narrow precincts of the ministry. In a religious career, it seemed to him, he would have to give up so much that he would greatly diminish or contract his life. Accordingly he began to teach in the Boston Latin School. But he soon realized that he was a complete failure. Greatly discouraged and now face to face again with what he should do as a life work, he decided to return to his earlier choice and prepare himself to be a minister. When he went to the Episcopal Theological Seminary at Alexandria, Virginia, he found his fellow students lacking the intellectual training and the culture to which he had been accustomed at Harvard, but he found something else he had missed before—a devout piety, a wholehearted dedication to the spiritual life, and a sense of divine fellowship. He did not abandon his previous culture; on the contrary, he added to it throughout his life, having a comprehensive knowledge of literature, an appreciation of the fine arts, and a love for travel rarely surpassed. Readers of his biography by Allen are made to feel on almost every page what a rich and abounding life he led even to the end; yet with all this culture he combined a rich spiritual life that made him the favorite preacher of all the universities of this country, a prophet in Israel. In other words, it is difficult to tell in his personality where culture ended and religion began; they became identical; they were fused in a rich and expanding life, dedicated entirely to the service of God and the relief of man's estate. His favorite text was, "I am come that they might have life, and that they might have it more abundantly."

With these two illustrations—Browning, a layman, many-sided, almost myriad-minded, and yet always ready to give a reason for the Christian faith to which he held; and Phillips Brooks, a preacher and prophet who found all the

22

paths that lead to God—we realize that there need not be any conflict between culture and religion.

II

I suppose the best known definition of culture is Matthew Arnold's: "a harmonious expansion of all the powers which make the beauty and worth of human nature." To add his shorter expressions, which he used with discomforting frequency, culture is "sweetness and light," "the pursuit of perfection." He also adapted two other expressions: Montesquieu's "to render an intelligent being yet more intelligent" and Bishop Wilson's "to make reason and the will of God prevail." If one takes all of these expressions together and understands them in the sense of Arnold, he will see that culture is something more than the development of the mind, or the love of the fine arts, or refinement. It meant for Arnold the development of all the four powers of intellect, social life and manners, love of beauty, and conduct—all harmoniously developed and everlastingly expanded.

Thomas Henry Huxley had the same broad view of education and culture, as may be seen in his essay "Science and Culture." He certainly included the aesthetic and the moral, though he was not so sensitive to religious values as was Arnold. Consider the key paragraph of his address on "A Liberal Education":

That man, I think, has had a liberal education who has been so trained in youth that his body is the ready servant of his will, and does with ease and pleasure all the work that, as a mechanism, it is capable of; whose intellect is a clear, cold, logic engine, with all its parts of equal strength, and in smooth working order; ready, like a steam engine, to be turned to any kind of work, and spin the gossamers as well as forge the anchors of the mind;

23

whose mind is stored with a knowledge of the great and fundamental truths of Nature and of the laws of her operations; one
who, no stunted ascetic, is full of life and fire, but whose passions are trained to come to heel by a rigorous will, the servant
of a tender conscience; who has *learned to love all beauty,
whether of Nature or of art, to hate all vileness, and to respect
others as himself.*

In other words, both culture and religion emphasize the
total man rather than the one-sided man. One of the perils of
our modern life, and especially of education, is that we have
become extreme specialists. It is well known what effects
the division of labor has had on the laboring population—
men working on small parts of great machines—all that we
mean by mass production. Now even more detrimental has
been the tendency to make out of men mere fractions of
humanity. We consider the physical man, the economic man,
the scientific man, the political man, the social man, the
aesthetic man, rather than the total man, the rich and
abounding personality. One of the dangers of extreme specialization is that we forget our human relationships and
we neglect our human inheritance.

III

In the life of the whole man, whether we think of culture
or religion, we need to emphasize the place of right thinking, wise thinking. In what was perhaps the most celebrated
address ever made at Harvard, Emerson defined the scholar
as "Man Thinking." He did not have in mind the philosopher, but rather the graduates of our American colleges
and universities. He had in mind the man who saturates
politics with thought, religion with thought, who brings

thought to bear upon business problems or scientific research.

Cardinal Newman had the same thing in mind when he spoke of the intellect "which knows, and thinks while it knows"—in other words, the man who studies, and thinks while he studies; reads, and thinks while he reads; travels, and thinks while he travels; lives or experiences, and thinks of the process through which he is passing. It cannot be emphasized too much that right thinking is just as important as right living, and that loose thinking is just as fatal as loose living. If we adopt the idea of the total man, then it inevitably follows that the moral obligation to be intelligent is just as great as the moral obligation to be good. Thinking is something more than the accumulation of information or knowledge; it rises above whatever is contemplated and sees it in relation to other things. Anyone who makes a collection of passages in the wisdom literature of the Bible will realize the large place that wisdom has in revelation. The eighth chapter of Proverbs is but one of many superb passages.

To think, one must have a well-trained and disciplined mind, the characteristics of which are: the capacity for hard work, concentration, accuracy, clearness, memory. No amount of piety or inspiration can take its place. Such a mind demands infinite patience and is never fully disciplined. "The joy of elevated thoughts" is one of the supreme satisfactions of life, the wisdom that passes all understanding, the enlargement of mind that issues in the illumination of soul. Such a mind is free of prejudice, open-minded, alert to receive new impressions and new ideas. Intellectual curiosity is one of the rarest virtues. Such a mind is free to follow truth wherever it may lead. It is opposed to inhibitions. taboos, censorship, and legislation that tends to curb the man in his laboratory or in his library.

IV

Let me call attention to some of the most common fallacies in thinking. They have their bearing on religion as well as on education. We tend to generalize too quickly and on inadequate knowledge of facts. The art of making distinctions or of discrimination is the beginning of wisdom. The man who does not discriminate between various types of people within nationalities or races may make fatal mistakes in his judgments. John Morley said that labels are devices for saving talkative people the trouble of thinking. Here is the basis of all sorts of prejudice. There are Englishmen and Englishmen, Jews and Jews, Negroes and Negroes, Southerners and Southerners, Northerners and Northerners, yes, Germans and Germans. There is always a chance for surprises in the wider knowledge of people, unexpected revelations from sources that have been closed to us by insufficient knowledge. The man who does not discriminate between the working rich and the idle rich, or between the constructive labor leader and a walking delegate, may fail to understand the industrial problem.

We need constantly to examine more closely the meanings of words, for most of our disagreements come out of false conceptions and definitions. We need to discriminate between sentimentalism and sentiment, intellectualism and wisdom, reason in its limited sense and reason in its exalted sense, efficiency that is crude and unlightened and effectiveness that organizes and harmonizes, ecclesiasticism and Christianity, faith that contradicts reason and faith that transcends reason, jingoism and patriotism, knowledge and wisdom, illusion and vision, the pseudo-classic and the classic, eccentricity and originality, pedantry and scholarship, fancy and imagination, sectionalism and regionalism, utopian idealism and practical idealism. Just as the cultivation of the five senses leads to delicate distinctions in sensibility, so the right use of words, the feeling for shades of distinction, is one of the gates to the palace of wisdom.

One of the most disappointing things about seemingly well-educated people is that they do not know how to react from one extreme without going to the other. Many college graduates are just as bad as people who never saw the inside of a college. It is quite common for college men to react from the point of view of their orthodox parents when they get a superficial idea of science or of the critical approach to religion. That is just what happened in the Victorian age when there were two extremes: a science that resulted in agnosticism or determinism, and a religion that resisted every scientific concept or hypothesis. The truth, of course, was in the adjustment or reconciliation of the new knowledge to the old faith, and this was made by many of the wisest people in England and America, but the supposed conflict comes out often in individuals or in whole regions.

If history teaches anything, it is that in every age there are two tendencies struggling for supremacy—the radical and the conservative—and that the truth is with neither. If the two forces get to be further and further apart we have inevitable revolution. "A plague o' both your houses!" is the slogan of men who believe in conservative progress and progressive conservatism.

V

A sense and appreciation of values goes beyond the intellectual discrimination of which we have been speaking. It involves good taste, refinement, good manners, sensibility. Both the humanist and the man of religious insight distinguish between quantity and quality, bigness and fineness, mass production of every type and the individual's or artisan's production. William James in a well-known essay defined the result of education as the sifting of human creations, the admiration of what is really admirable, the disesteem of what is cheap and trashy. "Our colleges," he said, "ought to have lit up in us a lasting relish for the better kind of man, a loss of appetite for mediocrity, and a disgust for cheapjacks." In his opinion the very calamity and shipwreck of a higher education is "to be unable to scent out human excellence, to know it only when ticketed and labelled and forced on us by others"—in other words, to be unable to know a good man when we see him, to distinguish between a charlatan and a gentleman, between a demagogue and a statesman; to know a good job when we see it, whether it be a bridge, a house, or a painting; to esteem the music of Beethoven, of Wagner, as compared with jazz; to see the difference between the poetry of Eddie Guest and that of Robert Frost; to feel the difference between books of the hour and books of all time. Such distinctions may affect character.

One of the essential phases in the sense of values is the choice between what is merely practical or useful and what contributes to the full development of personality. Here religion and culture have a common enemy. Many people are utilitarians or materialists who do not call themselves such, and utilitarianism as a system of ethics has been too largely dominant in America. What one really likes or prefers is a far more important element in character than most people think—and, still more important, what we ought to like, what we may come to like by the proper cultivation of mind and spirit.

VI

We may get more definitely at the meaning of culture, as Arnold and those who follow him conceive it, if we look further at those four powers which he enumerated and defined as the elements of culture. Arnold certainly did not underrate conduct as a factor in culture; for he made it three fourths of life, much to the discomfiture of some proponents of culture in its narrow aspects. Conduct he conceived of as righteousness, as morality. The great exponents of righteousness were the Hebrews and the Puritans, and to them he pays constant tribute, especially when he compares their principles and achievements with those of people who have failed to pay due heed to conduct. Time and again, he says, the world has had to return to morality and righteousness in periods of decadence or of skepticism or of sensual indulgence. No man, therefore, can be considered truly cultured who has not, as the foundation of his life, stern and rigid adherence to moral law. But Arnold gives another definition of conduct when he means by it the right ordering of one's life. A man may obey the Ten Commandments and meet all the requirements of a formal religious ritual and dogma, and yet fail because he lacks certain elements of stability, proportion, and balance that go to make up a rightly ordered life. It is not fair, therefore, to say that Arnold underrates conduct as a factor of life in the light

29

of either culture or religion when rightly understood. Here is where liberal education or humanism often fails; it is not concerned with making "reason and the will of God *prevail*."

As to the sense and appreciation of beauty as an element in culture all would agree, but it is not so often related to religion. By beauty we mean symmetry, balance, form, in contrast with ugliness, which means deformity, lopsidedness, confusion, chaos. Space does not allow at this point the application of this idea to nature or the fine arts; but we all ought to know what Keats meant when he said, "A thing of beauty is a joy for ever," or, "Beauty is truth, truth beauty," or what Emerson meant when he said, "Beauty is its own excuse for being," or what Sidney Lanier meant when he spoke of the "holiness of beauty."

The psalmist speaks of the beauty of the Lord. If we would be Godlike, then, we ought to realize how much beauty there is in the world that God created—surely he must love it and see that it is good because it is shot through with splendor and beauty. If we would be Christlike, we must think how much Christ suggested when he said, "Consider the lilies of the field," or when he found the deepest truths hidden in the common things of this earth. Whatever else Christ was, he was an artist; every word he ever uttered was a figure of speech or a parable. Need I suggest that the secret of the Psalms is in the blending of melody and artistic language with the spirit of devotion, and that Paul himself, with all his argumentative language, could now and then rise to such poetic language as we find in his epistles. The book of Job is not a theological treatise on the problem of sin and suffering, but a sublime drama or epic of the inner life. The great mistake of Puritanism was that it ignored the claims of beauty upon the human soul—that its followers mutilated great cathedrals, banished music from its forms of service, and reduced life to a certain hardness and rigidity. Arnold raised a pertinent question when he asked what Shakespeare would have done on the "Mayflower." The art of living—the greatest of all arts—is more than the art of thinking, or the purely emotional aspects of religion.

As to the power of social life and manners, we may claim that it is an essential factor in both culture and religion. Refinement, good manners, the art of conversation, the mingling with all sorts and conditions of men and women, the realization of what it may mean to be a member of a club or a society, the amenities and graces that go to make up life—surely all these lead to cultured and abundant personality. I have never believed that a boor or a clown is a worthy representative of God in pulpit or parish, nor do I think that a fanatic or a sentimentalist or a religious demagogue is the best exponent of the divine life. Have you ever thought of the difference between John the Baptist and Jesus? The Elizabethan dramatist who spoke of Jesus as the first gentleman of the world had in mind his delicate relationship to children and women. Jesus was no ascetic but lived in the currents of life about him.

Now to return to Arnold's definition of culture as the harmonious expansion of all these powers. Have we not seen that it is also a good definition of religion, of the abundant life? To save a man is to save all of him. The soul thinks, feels, acts. I do not see how anyone can escape the idea that it is a man's religious duty to develop his mind to its fullest capacity; from this standpoint a laboratory or a library may be a temple or a house of worship. It is a man's religious duty to develop an appreciation of beauty, and it is also his religious duty to know how to live with people, how to grow

31

in the graces and amenities of life. It is his religious duty not only to obey the moral law but so to order his life that it may become more and more a means of effective service for the world. If such an ideal is incapable of realization within the limitations of life, certainly to aspire toward such a life, to approximate it, ought to be a supreme motive power. The objection may be readily made that one must specialize in some one power or develop some one gift—that such specialization is characteristic of our modern life. Granted that one must concentrate on one particular field or profession, it yet remains true that all of us may find, in the right use of leisure, opportunity for the development of all these powers, with now and then a bright interval, a precious interlude, in which our souls are refreshed, recreated, and we have glimpses of mountain heights, moments of inspiration and transfiguration.

VII

What is the opposite of such a life, whether we think of it from the standpoint of culture or of religion? With Arnold the opposite of culture was the exclusion or the neglect of any one of these powers. Those who follow culture as an ideal are the children of light, God's chosen people; those who narrow their lives are Philistines. There are intellectual Philistines, men who magnify rationalism, technical scholarship, the scientific method at the expense of human values; artistic Philistines, who are followers of art for art's sake instead of art for art's and man's sake, who live in ivory towers or palaces of art or in strictly bohemian circles; social Philistines, the followers of conventions, social forms and fashions, out of touch with elemental and primitive virtues, sacrificing individuality and personality; and

Philistines of conduct, either those who are strict followers of the Puritans in their insistence upon the letter of a formal creed, or utilitarians, followers of Mammon, who interpret success in terms of material prosperity.

What Arnold meant by Philistinism, the Christian means by sin. If we are right in our premises, we must conclude that sin is anything that comes between us and the full development of the abundant life. The man who neglects to develop his intellect, who is thoughtless, indolent, muddle-headed, who fails to interpret for others the truths in which he believes, is a sinner. The man who is blind to the beauty of God's world, who is deaf to music, who has not some feeling for beauty of form and structure, who does not know something of that long effort of men to interpret God and man and the universe in terms of beauty, is a sinner. The man who lives an ascetic life, careless of his physical appearance or of his social relations with other men, who is not a gentleman in the truest sense of that word, is a sinner. The man who blunders through life, who arrives at a state of arrested development, who reaches the full maturity of his powers at middle age, is a sinner.

There seems to be no escape from the logic or the good sense of this point of view. We may all go to the mourners' bench on this proposition: we are all miserable sinners in the sight of God. We have all fallen short of the glory that has been revealed to us. Genuine humanism and genuine religion make demands upon us that we dare not ignore.

Another fundamental idea in Arnold and all other humanists is that the function of criticism is "a disinterested endeavour to learn and propagate the best that is known and thought in the world." Criticism establishes standards and values. It asks uncomfortable questions and makes comparisons that are not always conducive to self-complacency. Take any one of those four powers and compare our own limited realization of it with the best exponents of the power. And here is where literature is of a great service in revealing what these powers at their best, or the combination of them, can be. We have a clearer comprehension of the power of intellect if we know a Bacon, who took all knowledge to be his province, or a Thomas Huxley, whose clear-headed exposition has won him a place in creative literature as well as among scientific treatises. We can better understand the ideal of beauty if we read Plato, or the masters of the Renaissance, or Keats. Social life and manners take on a new light when we know the comedies of Shakespeare, the novels of Thackeray and Dickens, the satires of Swift, and our contemporary dramatists and novelists. The key to the understanding of moral or religious conduct may be found at the best in Bunyan, Milton, and Hawthorne. And all of them combined may be better realized in the personalities and writings of such comprehensive souls as Shakespeare, Goethe, and Browning.

VIII

I realize that, as we have already said, there has always been a conflict between some of the interpreters of culture and religion. It is a conflict that centers in the seemingly conflicting ideals of self-realization and self-sacrifice. These are the two voices that sound in each of us. Athens and Jerusalem were the two cities of light of the ancient world, and their civilizations emphasized respectively spontaneity of consciousness and strictness of conscience, sweetness and light and obedience to law, culture in its narrower sense and sin. The Renaissance and the Reformation were the reincarnations of these two ancient civilizations, and served to emphasize conflicting ideals. Eighteenth-century Deism with its emphasis on rationalism was followed by the Wesleyan revival. There has been a constant conflict from the beginning of our American history between universities that grew away from the ties that bound them to religious organizations and the churches which founded them. Harvard and the University of Virginia were attacked as centers of infidelity.

Several years ago I was asked by Dr. Robert Kelly, secretary of the Association of American Colleges, to write a paper on, "Does the modern educational process ignore religion, or combat religion, or does it develop religious attitudes and values?" It was a difficult question to answer. He had in mind the conflict that I have been suggesting, and more especially the conflict that had been continued in this period under different circumstances. Of the conflict between religion and science in the Victorian age I shall have more to say in the last chapter of this volume. Many contemporary scientists have insisted that everything must be judged from the scientific standpoint, that the only valid question about anything is, Is it scientific? that the only knowledge that is worth while is that which comes from observation or measurement, and that all other questions must be met with a frank and honest agnosticism. From Herbert Spencer to Harry Elmer Barnes there have been far too many investigators and teachers who have maintained an insolent attitude toward spiritual values. When Barnes exclaims that the discovery of certain amazing facts about Betelgeuse "blows sky-high the foundations of the whole set of moral conceptions of Judaism and Christianity" and when he asks, "Could anything be more satisfying as the ultimate reward of activity than the state of complete extinction in the chemical state known as death?" one does not wonder that there is a conflict between religion and science. When Clarence Darrow was put forth as the champion of the forces of enlightenment against Bryan as the leader of the Fundamentalists, one saw the aftermath of the debate between Thomas Huxley and Bishop Wilberforce.

We need to realize that the very greatest scientists of today are overthrowing the whole mechanistic and materialistic interpretation of man and the cosmic universe. I allude to such men as Eddington, Jeans, and Einstein in the realm of physics, and to the statement, written by Robert A. Millikan and signed by fifteen of the most prominent and representative scientists of this country, which says in memorable language: "The purpose of science is to develop a knowledge of the facts, the laws, and processes of nature. *The even more important function* of religion is to develop the consciences, the ideals, and aspirations of mankind. Each of these activities represents a deep and vital function of the soul of man, and both are necessary for the life, the progress, and the happiness of the human race."

There we have the basis for the harmonizing of science and religion. There is the same sort of contrast between extremists in psychology, such as John B. Watson, and the more moderate and better-balanced men of the type of William James, Angell, and McDougall, and between sociologists who have specialized in the abnormal specimens of humanity, the delinquents of society, to such an extent that they have lost sight of the higher social values, and such a scholar as Charles A. Ellwood, who in his *The Reconstruction of Religion* and *Man's Social Destiny* says that we shall not be able to reconstruct our civilization without the reconstruction of our religion, and that "religion is the summation of all our values, the vision of all things in the light of eternity."

Have we not sometimes felt that philosophy has abdicated its position as the synthesis of all knowledge and become the slave of the sciences? The philosophy of Haeckel and Bertrand Russell, the pragmatism of James as interpreted not by himself but by his followers and without regard to the import of some of his other writings, the instrumentalism of John Dewey, went far afield from the great tradition of Plato, Spinoza, and Kant. Just when the situation looked darkest, came Bergson, Eucken, and more recently Whitehead. The last has contended that nature cannot be divorced from its aesthetic values, that all the achievements of science have been built on the instinctive faith in a rational order of nature, and that a thoroughgoing evolutionary philosophy is inconsistent with materialism. He has laid the basis for religious faith in saying that "religion is the vision of something that stands beyond, behind, and within the passing flux of immediate things." "Apart from religion," he adds, "human life is a flash of occasional enjoyment lighting up a mass of pain and misery. . . . The worship of God is not a rule of safety—it is an adventure of the spirit. . . . Apart from God there would be no actual world. . . . He is the binding element in the world. The consciousness which is individual in us is universal in Him; the love which is partial in us is all-embracing in Him."

When we speak, then, of the conflict between culture and religion or between science and religion, we need constantly to bear in mind that it is a conflict between the extremists and the men of balance within each sphere of life and thought. There have been some humanists who have ignored religion as an element in humanism—men like Walter Lipp-

37

mann and Irving Babbitt—but there have been other humanists, such as Paul Elmer More and T. S. Eliot, who have
insisted that humanism and religion are identical in their
opposition to many of the currents of modern thought and
in their positive values. Some of us think of More as the
best-equipped critic America has had. As the author of the
Shelburne Essays he had a command of world literature
that no other critic has had. At the end of his life he under-
took a series of great studies of Platonism and Christianity.
There is every evidence that he started out with the conviction that the Platonic philosophy was the basis of what was
best in Christianity, but his volume entitled *Christ the Word*
is a profound statement of the value and authority of the
Incarnation as the fulfillment of all that was best in Plato's
ideas. He contended that "the two traditions together constitute the greatest effort of the human mind to find at once
an ultimate religion and philosophy." Plato would have
thought that Christianity gave precisely the one thing for
which he had been searching all his life. If he had heard
Jesus talk of the Father, he would doubtless have exclaimed,
"My Lord and my God!"

IX

This all-too-brief survey of tendencies in contemporary
life and thought gives emphasis to the main contention of
this chapter, that certain men have found a proper synthesis
of culture and religion. There have always been men and
even periods of history that have reconciled them. Plato
combined the moral earnestness of Socrates with the artistic
sense of the Greek dramatists. Isaiah was a prophet and also
a poet of the first rank. David was a warrior and a ruler but
also the writer of hymns who set going a wave of lyric

melody that persisted throughout Hebrew history. Michelangelo combined the strictness and severity of Savonarola and the artistic glory of Raphael. John Milton combined all the thirst of knowledge and love of beauty that made the Renaissance a period of splendor with the morality, the civic responsibility, the intense religious faith of the Reformation. John Wesley used the learning of Oxford as an aid to his world-wide revival of religion. Robert Browning summed up all the achievements of the Victorian age and at the same time expressed in many poems his faith in the Incarnation as the revelation of God's love. Robert E. Lee was a perfect Virginia gentleman, master of military strategy, tragic hero of the Confederacy, prophet and builder of the new South, and withal as Christlike a figure as ever trod the earth.

And beyond all these is Jesus himself, who, as we have seen, was a perfect realization of all the four powers of which we have been speaking, and in his life and in his death the Saviour and Redeemer of man. Well did Sidney Lanier write of him as the perfect crystal:

> But Thee, but Thee, O sovereign Seer of time,
> But Thee O poets' Poet, Wisdom's Tongue,
> But Thee, O man's best Man, O love's best Love,
> O perfect life in perfect labor writ,
> O all men's Comrade, Servant, King, or Priest,—
> What *if* or *yet,* what mole, what flaw, what lapse,
> What least defect or shadow of defect,
> What rumor, tattled by an enemy,
> Of inference loose, what lack of grace
> Even in torture's grasp, or sleep's, or death's,—
> Oh, what amiss may I forgive in Thee,
> Jesus, good Paragon, thou Crystal Christ?

39

CHAPTER II

CHAMPIONS OF THE MORAL LAW

A RECENTLY published book entitled *The Ten Commandments* is a symposium of short novels written by such distinguished writers as Thomas Mann, Rebecca West, Franz
Werfel, John Erskine, Bruno Frank, Jules Romains, André
Maurois, Sigrid Undset, Hendrik Willem van Loon, and
Louis Bromfield. The subtitle, "Hitler's War Against the
Moral Code," suggests the general theme of the book. Each
of these writers tells a story that illustrates the working out
in human characters and incidents of one of the Ten Commandments, showing how in various occupied countries the
results of the disobedience of these commandments by Hitler
and his cohorts have been disastrous for the people themselves and have recoiled upon the temporary victors.

The book grew out of the astounding words of Hitler as
reported by Herman Rauschning, who writes the preface to
the volume:

It is not merely a question of Christianity and Judaism. We
are fighting against the most ancient curse that humanity has
brought upon itself. We are fighting against the perversion of
our soundest instincts. Ah, the God of the deserts, that crazed,
stupid, vengeful, Asiatic despot with his powers to make laws!
That slavekeeper's whip! That devilish "Thou shalt, thou shalt!"
And that stupid "Thou shalt not." It's got to get out of our
blood, that curse from Mount Sinai! That poison with which

40

both Jews and Christians have spoiled and soiled the free, wonderful instincts of man and lowered them to the level of doglike fright. . . . The day will come when I shall hold up against these commandments the table of a new law. And history will recognize our movement as the great battle for humanity's liberation, a liberation from the curse of Mount Sinai, from the dark stammerings of nomads who could no more trust their own sound instincts, who could understand the divine only in the form of a tyrant who orders one to do the very things one doesn't like. This is what we are fighting against : the masochistic spirit of self-torment, the curse of so-called morals, idolized to protect the weak from the strong in the face of the immortal law of battle, the great law of divine nature. Against the so-called ten commandments, against them we are fighting.[1]

By way of contrast Thomas Mann recreates the personality of Moses and the circumstances under which were given on Mount Sinai the commandments that "could serve as fundamental precept, as the rock of human decency, to all the peoples of the earth." When Moses had explained them to the people and presented them as tablets engraven by him on the mountain and as dictated by Jehovah, he concluded with the words that may be applied to Hitler and his inevitable downfall:

But woe to the man who shall arise and speak: "They are no longer valid." Woe to him who teaches you: "Arise and get rid of them ! . . ." He shall be mighty and powerful, he shall sit upon a golden throne, and he shall be looked up to as the wisest of all. For he knows that the inclination of the human heart is evil, even in youth. But that is about all that he will know, and

---

[1] This and the following quotations from *The Ten Commandments,* edited by Armin L. Robinson, are used by permission of the publisher, Simon & Schuster, Inc.

he who knows only that is as stupid as the night and it would
be better for him never to have been born. . . . Blood shall flow
in torrents because of his black stupidity, so much blood that the
redness shall vanish from the cheeks of mankind. But then the
people shall hew down the monster—inevitably; for they can
do naught else. And the Lord says, I shall raise my foot and
shall trample him into the mire, to the bottom of the earth shall
I cast the blasphemer. . . . That the earth may again be the
earth, a vale of want, yes, but not a sty of depravity.

Thus we have the gauntlet thrown down by the greatest
of all German refugees at the feet of Adolf Hitler, a ringing
defiance of his power that seemed once unconquerable. The
other stories present artistically the great significance of
each of the commandments. They are an eloquent witness to
the fact that there is an everlasting struggle between good
and evil in the world; that, despite all the injustice and
oppression of evil forces, there is something inherently good
in the heart of man which enables him to endure suffering
with heroism; that the very universe in the long run is hostile
to evil; and that the good eventually triumphs in the soul
of man made in the image of God and, let us believe, in the
final destiny of mankind.

II

It is not in Germany alone that the moral law is ignored
and repudiated. There is danger on the home front as well.
Do we really believe that "whatsoever a man soweth, that
shall he also reap"? Are the prophets of God still able to say,
"Thus saith the Lord"? Is there a moral law written upon
the very adamant of the earth? I shall not attempt more
than to suggest the tendencies of our modern life and thought
that weaken this faith in a moral order. Some interpreters

42

of modern science have accepted the seeming conclusion that we are all in the grip of cosmic forces over which we have no control, that either chance or a blind fate determines the nature of individual man and the rise and fall of nations, that the individual is not therefore responsible for his deeds, that the whole history of man is but the repetition of the cycle of the rise and fall of races and nations, and that time is but "a maniac scattering dust" and life but "a Fury slinging flame."

No one who has taught young men and women during the past twenty-five years can fail to have witnessed the revolt against conventions of all kinds, against such outworn ideals as duty and service, against what are called taboos and inhibitions of every kind. The most popular psychology for a decade deplored all suppression of urges. The lid was off. Restraint was considered a vice. The cult of smartness sought to enthrone the wisecrack as the acme of human wisdom. Many writers of real genius have contributed to the disillusionment and cynicism of the novel and the drama. What is morality? What is the good life? What is truth? All were asked with the sneer of a Mephistopheles or a Pilate.

Even in the midst of the Victorian age the reaction against moral standards had set in. Arthur Hugh Clough in "The Latest Decalogue" suggests a modern version of the Commandments which strikes at the heart of much modern life:

> Thou shalt have one God only; who
> Would be at the expense of two?
>
> No graven images may be
> Worship'd, except the currency:

43

Swear not at all; for, for thy curse
Thine enemy is none the worse:

At church on Sunday to attend
Will serve to keep the world thy friend:

Honour thy parents; that is, all
From whom advancement may befall;

Thou shalt not kill; but needst not strive
Officiously to keep alive:

Do not adultery commit;
Advantage rarely comes of it:

Thou shalt not steal; an empty feat,
Where 'tis so lucrative to cheat:

Bear not false witness; let the lie
Have time on its own wings to fly:

Thou shalt not covet, but tradition
Approves all forms of competition.

Rudyard Kipling, who in his "Recessional," reminded the British of their inheritance of the moral law and wrote in flaming words of the danger of haughty and unrighteous imperialism, later reinforced the idea with a less well-known poem, "The Gods of the Copybook Headings," by which he meant those fundamental maxims born out of the experience of the race if not handed down from Sinai. Over against the "Gods of the Copybook Headings" have always been the "Gods of the Market Place."

On the first Feminian Sandstones we were promised the Fuller
    Life
(Which started by loving our neighbor and ended by loving his
    wife)

44

Till our women had no more children and the men lost reason
and faith,
And the Gods of the Copybook Headings said, *"The Wages of
Sin is Death."*

And they had to explain it to every generation:

As it will be in the future, it was at the birth of Man
There are only four things certain since Social Progress began:—
That the Dog returns to his Vomit and the Sow returns to her
Mire;
And the burnt Fool's bandaged finger goes wabbling back to the
Fire;

And that after this is accomplished, and the brave new world
begins
When all men are paid for existing and no man must pay for his
sins,
As surely as Water will wet us, as surely as Fire will burn,
The Gods of the Copybook Headings with terror and slaughter
return![2]

What I am trying to set forth in this chapter is that the
greatest English writers, indeed the greatest of them all, are
the champions of the idea that there is a moral law, a moral
order, and that to sin against it is to bring remorse, retribu-
tion, and defeat upon individuals and upon nations. Let us
not deceive ourselves; we cannot ignore the terrible facts of
sin, of injustice, of oppression, of disease, of poverty, of
moral corruption. If we were ever inclined so to do, we
have been chastened and overwhelmed by the conditions that
now prevail around the whole earth. If one could bring to his

[2] From *Rudyard Kipling's Verse: Definitive Edition.* By permission of
the poet's daughter, Mrs. George Bambridge, and of Doubleday, Doran
& Co.

consciousness all the ravages of evil forces rampant in this world today and the suffering that the good are everywhere passing through, if for a moment his imagination could make all this chaos live in his mind, it would break his heart. This is no time for Pollyanna optimism, no time to quote Pope's famous words, "Whatever is, is right," or the song of Pippa,

> God's in his heaven—
> All's right with the world!

Even in ordinary times men have been impressed with the difference between the ideal and the real. Quote as fervidly as you may Hamlet's apostrophe to man—"What a piece of work is a man! How noble in reason! How infinite in faculty! In form and moving how express and admirable! In action how like an angel! In apprehension how like a god!" —but remember that the quotation ends with, "this quintessence of dust," and that there are many lines and phrases throughout the play that suggest that "the time is out of joint," that "something is rotten in the state of Denmark," and that this world is "stale, flat, and unprofitable." Quote Wordsworth,

> She was a Phantom of delight. . . .
> A perfect Woman, nobly planned,

but remember also that a later poet wrote about "the female of the species." Read Macaulay's panegyrics about the triumphs of democracy and industrialism in England and America, but read, by way of contrast, Edwin Markham's "The Man with the Hoe." Nature does not always inspire a sense of "something far more deeply interfused," but rather seems "red in tooth and claw" as it manifests itself in storms and floods, deserts and jungles, and all-devouring germs. Is history to be summed up in Tennyson's "one increasing purpose" or rather in the pessimistic motif that sounds through Byron's *Childe Harold,* in which the ruins of empires and nations pass before us suggesting the endless repetition of cycles from freedom to barbarism?

III

The development of Puritanism is one of the best illustrations of the everlasting struggle between good and evil. Certainly Puritan leaders or followers, with all their faith in God and in the invisible forces of good, did not minimize the evil in their own hearts, in the world in which they lived, and in the invisible world of devils and witches. They were good fighters—always. With all their defects and limitations we owe to them significant contributions to English civilization. Cromwell and his Ironsides defeated forever in England the theory and the practice of the divine right of kings and laid the foundation of parliamentary government. Everywhere in Europe there was a reversion to absolute monarchy, but the peaceable revolution of 1688 confirmed what the Puritans had established by violence. They made impossible the return to Catholicism at a time when the Counter Reformation was triumphant in Europe. They broke the tyranny of the Established Church and paved the way to religious tolerance, even though they themselves became intolerant when in power. In an extreme way they purified the social life of England at a time when social customs, the theater, the court, and the aristocracy had become decadent and corrupt. Above all, they magnified the individual's responsibility for his moral conduct. Their motto was not "I think, therefore I am" but "I believe, therefore I can."

This historic movement, which had its continuation in New England and in the Scotch-Irish groups of the South, found expression in John Bunyan and John Milton, and in this country in Nathaniel Hawthorne. *The Pilgrim's Progress,* considered by some a theological or moral treatise, merely a collection of innumerable texts from the Bible, is not only the greatest allegory ever written, but a human document filled with terse characterizations of all types of human nature, dramatic scenes and incidents, and a story that will enthrall anyone who gives it proper attention. It is one of the miracles of literature that its author was an illiterate tinker who knew only one book, but knew that Book so well that it enters into the warp and woof of this idiomatic, vital, and gripping volume. Bernard Shaw, who hates Puritanism in all its forms and ways, said that certain scenes in *Pilgrim's Progress* are as dramatic as any in Shakespeare.

What we are concerned with now is Bunyan's representation of the struggle between good and evil forces. His *Grace Abounding* gives the successive stages through which he passed in attaining his salvation. No man ever took such infinite pains to be sure that he was saved; no man ever conceived more vividly the besetting sins that attack one in his long, upward passage from death to life. What he actually experienced is lifted into real art in *Pilgrim's Progress.* Life as a journey along the road from the City of Destruction to the Land of Beulah has been used by many authors, but no one has named the places with greater accuracy and vividness than Bunyan—the Slough of Despond, the House of the Interpreter, the Hill Difficulty, the Palace Beautiful, the Valley of Humiliation, Vanity Fair, Doubting Castle, the Delectable Mountains, the River of Death, the

48

Heavenly City. The characters, to the casual reader mere abstractions, are instinct with life, limned with biting phrases: Worldly-wise Man, Facing Both-ways, Great Heart, Faint Heart, Ignorance, Apollyon, the jury in Vanity Fair, Giant Despair, the shepherds on the Delectable Mountains, Faithful, Hopeful.

Just one illustration will serve to show Bunyan's power of characterization and his dramatic handling of an incident. It is the jury of Vanity Fair that sits in judgment on Faithful:

Then went the jury out, whose names were Mr. Blindman, Mr. No-good, Mr. Malice, Mr. Love-lust, Mr. Live-loose, Mr. Heady, Mr. High-mind, Mr. Enmity, Mr. Liar, Mr. Cruelty, Mr. Hate-light, and Mr. Implacable; who every one gave in his private verdict against him among themselves, and afterwards unanimously concluded to bring him in guilty before the judge. And first among themselves, Mr. Blindman the foreman, said, I see clearly that this man is a heretic. Then said Mr. No-good, Away with such a fellow from the earth. Aye, said Mr. Malice, for I hate the very looks of him. Then said Mr. Love-lust, I could never endure him. Nor I, said Mr. Live-loose, for he would always be condemning my way. Hang him, hang him, said Mr. Heady. A sorry scrub, said Mr. High-mind. My heart riseth against him, said Mr. Enmity. He is a rogue, said Mr. Liar. Hanging is too good for him, said Mr. Cruelty. Let us despatch him out of the way, said Mr. Hate-light. Then said Mr. Implacable, Might I have all the world given me, I could not be reconciled to him; therefore let us forthwith bring him in guilty of death.

And so they did; therefore he was presently condemned to be had from the place where he was, to the place from whence he came, and there to be put to the most cruel death that could be invented.

49

Here, then, in the most realistic and idealistic forms, we have a representation of life and the forces that are struggling for supremacy. It is a grim, hard struggle, like the fight with Apollyon, but there are compensations all along the way, the triumphs of the spirit of man over all obstacles and evil forces.

IV

Nathaniel Hawthorne, who in his youth pored over the old Puritan volumes and listened to the strange tales that were handed down from generation to generation in the old witch-haunted town of Salem, wrote a short story called "The Celestial Railroad" in which he gave the modern substitute for *Pilgrim's Progress*. Living at a time when the renaissance of New England had come to its full flowering —a time of increasing wealth and culture—he reminded the readers of Emerson that all this prosperity and this reaction against Calvinism, all this ignoring of sin as a fact in human nature, might lead to a softness that would undermine civilization. The twilight of secret sin was to him a better symbol of man than the dawn of the emancipated mind. So he presents, very much in the manner of Bunyan, a celestial railroad from the City of Destruction to the Heavenly City. The gay crowd, as if going on a holiday, buy their tickets, check their baggage—symbolic of their burden of sins—straight through so that they won't have to bother about it any more, and sing merrily as they contemplate a safe transit. The engineer is Beelzebub or Apollyon or Satan; the conductor is Mr. Smooth-it-away. Just as the starting signal is given they see two pilgrims— Bunyan's very characters—starting out the hard way with their burdens on their backs. They call to them to come and board the train and thus avoid the long perilous journey, but the pilgrims heed not their invitation. After a while the lightning express train to Heaven pulls up at Vanity Fair, where the passengers become so engrossed with the fashions and shows and customs of that city that they forget where they are going and stay a long time—long enough for the two pilgrims to catch up with them and to be mocked at their trial. In fact the passengers unite in their persecution. Finally it occurs to them that they had better resume their journey, and they arrive at the River of Death only to find that there is no bridge. In their bewilderment they see coming out of the waters on the other side the two pilgrims, and they catch something of the Hallelujah song that welcomes them to the Celestial City.

Thus did Hawthorne, in Bunyan's own way, suggest the dangers of forgetting that the struggle with evil is an ever-present fact. In all of his novels and in many of his short stories, notably "The Minister's Black Veil" and "Ethan Brand," he deals with open and secret sin. *The Scarlet Letter* is a most impressive representation of the effects of the violation of the moral law on Arthur, Hester, their daughter Pearl, and Roger Chillingworth. The letter *A,* which is placed on Hester's bosom by an outraged community, is symbolic of her breaking of the seventh commandment, but it is not so terrible a fact as the letter *A* that is gradually burned on the bosom of her lover, who is the beloved minister of the church. Secret sin is punished even more severely than confessed sin. There is no greater passage in American fiction than the words of Arthur as he reveals his sin:

"People of New England!" cried he, with a voice that rose over them, high, solemn, and majestic—yet always a tremor through it, and sometimes a shriek, struggling up out of a fathomless depth of remorse and woe—"ye, that have loved me! ye, that have deemed me holy!—behold me here, the one sinner of the world! At last!—at last!—I stand upon the spot where, seven years since, I should have stood; here with this woman, whose arm, more than the little strength wherewith I have crept hitherward, sustains me, at this dreadful moment, from grovelling down upon my face! Lo, the scarlet letter which Hester wears! Ye have all shuddered at it? Wherever her walk hath been—wherever, so miserably burdened, she may have hoped to find repose—it hath cast a lurid gleam of awe and horrible repugnance round about her. But there stood one in the midst of you, at whose brand of sin and infamy ye have not shuddered!"

It seemed, at this point, as if the minister must leave the remainder of his secret undisclosed. But he fought back the bodily weakness—and, still more, the faintness of heart—that was striving for the mastery with him. He threw off all assistance, and stepped passionately forward a pace before the woman and the child.

"It was on him!" he continued, with a kind of fierceness; so determined was he to speak out the whole. "God's eye beheld it! The angels were forever pointing at it! The Devil knew it well, and fretted it continually with the touch of his burning finger! But he hid it cunningly from men, and walked among you with the mien of a spirit, mournful, because so pure in a sinful world!—and sad, because he missed his heavenly kindred! Now, at the death-hour he stands up before you! He bids you look again at Hester's scarlet letter! He tells you, that with all its mysterious horror, it is but the shadow of what he bears on his own breast, and that even this, his own red stigma, is no more than the type of what has seared his inmost heart! Stand any here that question God's judgment on a sinner? Behold! Behold a dreadful witness of it!"

Even worse is the plight of the husband who, with grave malignity, rejoices in the punishment that comes to those who have wronged him. To be sure the suffering of the two main characters has its purifying effect: Hester becomes a ministering angel in the community, and Arthur finds peace at last in the confession of his sin to the public. Puritanism has, with Hawthorne, become somewhat humanized, but the whole story is a dramatic representation of the consequences of sin and of the triumph of good over sin.

The House of Seven Gables is a powerful representation of the sin that follows its victims from generation to generation. Even in *The Marble Faun,* which has its setting in Rome, the bleak wind of the New England conscience blows through the novel. Somewhere in the background of the principal character there is a secret and mysterious sin, the effects of which cannot be put aside. Entangled with these voyagers from New England is a faunlike spirit living on the borderland between the animal and the human world— half faun, half man—who from his state of innocence passes into the consciousness of sin that haunts the woman he loves and eventually leads to his own desolation.

V

But it is in Milton that the struggles between the evil and the good forces of the world and of the cosmic universe, and more especially the struggle between the Royalists and the Puritans, find their greatest expression. Now Milton was a much more complex personality than the label Puritan would indicate. He was the most highly cultured man of his age, the climax of all that we mean by the Renaissance. By inheritance, by long years of study at Cambridge and in Horton, by his travels abroad when the academies of Italy were still flourishing, he had come into possession of the traditions of classical and modern culture. In his early years he wrote a masque, *Comus,* and in his last years he wrote a tragedy, *Samson Agonistes,* thus excelling in forms of literature that were generally condemned by the Puritans. His plea for the freedom of the mind in *Areopagitica* went far beyond the narrow intellectual limits of the faction with which he had aligned himself. His mastery of poetic technique places him among the great poets of the world, far removed from men like Bunyan and Cromwell, the two other chief representatives and exponents of Puritanism.

When all is said, however, it remains true that Milton was for many years identified with the Puritan cause. First of all, his life was free from all the stains that marked so many of the Cavaliers and Royalists; it was a poem in itself, a "pattern of the best and noblest things." He was from the first a dedicated spirit and lived "as ever in my great Taskmaster's eye." There was nothing of that struggle between the worldly and the spiritual elements of man's nature that we find in John Donne. To trace his development is to find him becoming more and more severe in his morality, more and more conscious of the struggles of his day.

In *Comus* we have represented in a very artistic way the conflict between Comus and his crew—representatives of that luxury, frivolity, and licentiousness that were regnant in the life of the court—and the lady and her two brothers—representatives of that purity and seriousness of life which increasingly characterized the Puritan faction. This social conflict had not yet assumed the extreme quality that later characterized it, but there is here the spirit that finally closed the theaters, abolished the maypole, instituted the blue laws, and made even innocent mirth ashamed to show itself.

In "Lycidas," along with the wealth of allusion that links it with the pastoral poetry of Greece, there is heard the note of the coming conflict between the Established Church and the Puritans. While Milton had grown up in an orthodox Anglican family and had even contemplated entering the ministry, he became more and more convinced that the Anglican clergy were so corrupt that only the abolition of the episcopacy would bring about a better condition. He was not willing to subscribe himself "slave" by taking on the vows of the church. So in his indictment of the clergy in "Lycidas" one hears the trumpet of the coming battle. They were ignorant, selfish, corrupt; and they were leading England back into the Roman Church. With all his righteous indignation, anticipating the meeting of Parliament once more, he exclaims:

> But that two-handed engine at the door
> Stands ready to smite once, and smite no more.

He was no better satisfied with the Presbyterian Church that had been established under the direction of Calvin and his followers; for it too sought to impose its form of organization and creed upon all the people of England. "New *Presbyter* is but old Priest writ large." The Presbyterians had no sooner come into power in Parliament than they passed a bill which established a censorship over books, and this stirred Milton to write the greatest plea for intellectual freedom in our language. Evil here took the form of proscription, prohibition, oppression. The good cause was associated with freedom of thought and expression.

When he heard the news of the persecution of the Protestants in Piedmont, Italy—the first Protestants of Europe even when other countries were worshiping idols—he wrote a sonnet which blazed with indignation and prophecy:

Avenge, O Lord, thy slaughtered Saints, whose bones
Lie scattered on the Alpine mountains cold.

The sonnet, which had been for Elizabethan poets the medium for the expression of love, became a trumpet in his hands.

Thus for twenty years Milton was wholeheartedly engaged in the struggle between the Puritans and the Royalists. He could not think of himself as traveling abroad or as living in an ivory tower; he could not "praise a fugitive and cloistered virtue" when tyranny and oppression were seeking to enslave his people. From seeing the struggle for religious liberty he passed to a visualization of it as a struggle for political freedom. As the secretary to Cromwell, he followed in detail every incident of the Civil War; he could hear the shout of Cromwell to his soldiers on various battlefields, "Let God arise, let his enemies be scattered." He even defended the execution of Charles I because he felt that the king could no longer be trusted to keep his word, and was therefore a persistent enemy to a free government.

He rejoiced in the victory that came with the establishment of the Protectorate, but he immediately warned Cromwell and Fairfax that the days of peace made necessary a still further struggle.

Peace hath her victories
No less renowned than War.

The new foes that he saw arising were connected with an established church, of whatever kind it might be, and with the effort to restrain individual freedom.

Milton's pamphlets make up a large portion of his writings; they are not easy reading, but there are passages which are as sublime as any English prose. Especially outstanding among all these pamphlets is the *Areopagitica,* his impassioned plea for intellectual freedom. It ranks with the treatment of the same theme by John Locke, John Stuart Mill, and Thomas Jefferson. Declaring that censorship had its origin in the Spanish Inquisition, and attributing the greatness of the English people to their freedom from such inquisitions or censorship, he pleaded with Parliament not to destroy this tradition and not to make impossible his vision of "a noble and puissant nation rousing herself like a strong man after sleep, and shaking her invincible locks." It would take many people to build the temple of truth and knowledge —men of every point of view and every temperament.

For a brief period Milton rejoiced in the triumph of what he called the "good old cause." It seemed as if God had come to the aid of his followers in all the fields of human endeavor. Then the test of his faith came with the death of Cromwell, the weak Protectorate that followed, and the restoration of the king in 1660. To a man who felt so intensely the struggle through which a noble people had passed, it might well seem that the loathsome opposite of all that he had dreamed and worked for had come to pass. The Restoration period in English history was characterized by Milton when he spoke of having "fallen on evil days, . . . and evil tongues," of being "with dangers compassed round, and solitude," and of hearing "the barbarous dissonance of Bacchus and his revellers." Comus and his crew now dominated the social life. The church was in alliance with a corrupt monarchy; the bodies of the heroes whom the poet had celebrated hung upon the gibbets; and the vision of a free commonwealth which he had written even as the king was returning had vanished like the baseless fabric of a dream. Milton himself was in danger of death, for it is one of the miracles that one who had written such violent things during the struggle should have escaped the fury of the victors. Crowning his sufferings was his blindness; he could see neither nature nor the books which had been the solace and inspiration of his life, nor "human face divine." And yet in spite of all the difficulties and disappointments Milton rose to the heights of courage and faith. At a time when he might have uttered the cry, "My God, my God, why hast thy forsaken me?" he wrote instead:

> Yet I argue not
> Against Heaven's hand or will, nor bate a jot
> Of heart or hope, but still bear up and steer
> Right onward.

To him may be applied the last words he wrote concerning the fall and triumph of Samson:

> Samson hath quit himself
> Like Samson, and heroicly hath finished
> A life heroic, on his enemies
> Fully revenged. . . .
>
> . . . .
>
> Nothing is here for tears, nothing to wail
> Or knock the breast; no weakness, no contempt,
> Dispraise, or blame; nothing but well and fair,
> And what may quiet us in a death so noble.
>
> . . . .
>
> All is best, though we oft doubt
> What the unsearchable dispose
> Of Highest Wisdom brings about
> And ever best found in the close.
> Oft He seems to hide his face,
> But unexpectedly returns,
> And to his faithful Champion hath in place

Bore witness gloriously; when Gaza mourns,
And all that band them to resist
His uncontrollable intent.
His servants He, with new acquist
Of true experience from this great event,
With peace and consolation hath dismissed,
And calm of mind, all passion spent.

VI

The most remarkable thing is that under all these circumstances Milton should have retained his creative imagination, for few men have written great poetry after they were fifty. He literally flung into the face of the victorious court and their supporters the epic of Puritanism; he would at least triumph in the realm of art. I cannot, of course, deal at any length with *Paradise Lost,* a poem which Mark Twain had in mind when he said that a classic is something that everybody is expected to have read and nobody reads. In spite of all the indifference of the general reader and the jests that have been directed to it by critics, I still maintain that the reading of the poem may well be an event in any man's life. It must be admitted that much of the poem requires the utmost patience. There are sometimes long stretches of prosaic and didactic language, especially those passages in which "God argues like a school divine." The theological point of view which few of us still hold, the physical background of the universe, the severity and sometimes hardness that one feels as characteristic of the treatment of both the human and the divine characters—all leave us cold. Many who do not care about any of these elements of the poem are yet extravagant in their praise of the grand style in which it is written—the majesty and the sublimity of its verse that caused Tennyson to call Milton "God-gifted organ-voice of England," and Wordsworth to say, "Thou hadst a voice whose sound was like the sea."

What we are most concerned about is Milton's representation of the struggle between good and evil and his treatment of the moral law. Granting all that has been said about the temporary phases of the poem, it yet remains true that he visualized and felt intensely the fact of sin and its effect on the universe and on man. If he did not succeed in justifying the ways of God to man, and especially in explaining the origin of evil, he yet gave a picture, told a story that goes beyond Bunyan and Hawthorne in causing us to realize the power, the destructiveness, the subtlety, even the charm, of evil, and of evil not only as related to the individual but as related to infinity and eternity. To Milton evil was not an abstraction; it was incarnated in the character and personality of Satan, who is no medieval devil with horns and forked tail, but a towering figure—an archangel a little damaged, the sun in eclipse. First a rebel against God's decrees, he becomes the commander of Hell and its inmates. Speaking words of eloquence, overcoming despair with courage, defeat with victory, he is ready to use every power to thwart the plans of God, later using upon Eve the subtlety, the sophistry, and the charm of the tempter. With him are associated: Moloch, the embodiment of brute force and violence; Mammon, who sees the vision of enchanted palaces that may be built even in Hell; Belial, whose tongue

> Dropt manna, and could make the worst appear
> The better reason,

the forerunner of all the sophistical thinkers and demagogues of history; Beelzebub, whose look drew audience and whose eloquence won the hosts of Hell to support the plan for the temptation of man; and, along with these, Sin and Death, allegorical figures who sum up in themselves the most potent enemies of man, and who, after the Fall, spread discord and evil throughout the universe.

If Milton saw evil in these incarnate forms, he also saw the good forces of the universe as represented in God, Christ, the archangels, the hosts of angels, and Adam and Eve in their state of innocence in the newly created Garden of Eden. Perhaps it may be said that Milton saw and felt more intensely the evil forces because he had struggled with them in his own age. Those portions of the poem which are most generally read are the first two books, in which Satan and his hosts in Hell are represented in their most splendid forms and expressions. Those who go beyond these portions, however, will find compensation in the gradual degradation and final overthrow of Satan and in the reconciliation and redemption of Adam and Eve. The panorama of history, which is outlined by Michael for Adam, closes with the triumph of the Redeemer.

When one has yielded as much as possible to the criticism of the cosmology and theology of the poem, it remains one of the best symbols of individual man that we have in literature. We may agree, if we accept the theory of evolution, that man began at a stage just above the animal and not as a perfect being; but he still lives on the earth, surrounded, as in Milton's pictorial imagination, by chaos. Beneath him is Hell, to which he may go easily on the bridge that has been built by Sin and Death to facilitate his descent; but the earth and the universe are suspended from Heaven by a golden chain, and there is a ladder upon which he can mount to the battlements of Heaven. Reduce this to whatever intellectual terms you may, it is a perfect symbol of the powers that fight for supremacy in the soul of man. If the human race as a whole did not fall with Adam and thereby incur the curse of original sin, the individual man is always in danger of falling from the innocence of childhood. If the explanation of evil is not to be found in Satan, or any other type of personal devil, if we accept the influences of heredity and environment as sufficient explanation of the fall or failure of man, it yet remains true that there is something in the very nature of the cosmic universe and of man that is allied with invisible forces of evil.

That struggle, from the standpoint of psychology, is better represented in *Paradise Regained*. Here we have the battle fought out between two individuals—Christ and Satan. To be sure, we have the suggestion of Satan's council with his allies, who have been busy ever since the Fall creating false religions and standards, and also a suggestion that heavenly beings are concerned in the struggle. But in the main it is the testing of the values of life. It is a striking fact that Milton selected the Temptation rather than the Crucifixion as the event of central importance in the life of Christ. As Adam fell through temptation, Christ triumphed over it. As presented by Milton this temptation was not a farce. Here is the young man standing upon the threshold of what he thinks of as a divine mission. The prophets who foresaw him as the Messiah, his mother, the disciples who have been drawn to him at his baptism, and he himself, now hungry and desolate in the desert, have thought much about his relation to his own people as being that one who would restore them from the tyranny of Rome. The three temptations are calculated to focus the problem. To the first he says, "Man shall not live by bread alone"; to the second, in which Satan sets forth with much ingenuity the power that had made possible the splendor of Roman civilization and the wisdom and culture of Greek civilization, he replies that his kingdom is to be one in which spiritual values shall eventually win the victory; and to the third, in which Satan tempts him to use magic as a means of showing his divinity, he replies, as he did so often when even his disciples sought signs and wonders, that he was in the hands of God.

Everywhere, then, in Milton—in his prose as well as in his poetry—we have life represented as a struggle between good and evil, righteousness and sin, God and Satan, Milton and the dark forces that were potent and regnant in his age. He deserves the praise accorded the seraph Abdiel, who resisted the temptation to join Satan's rebellion in Heaven:

Servant of God, well done! Well hast thou fought
The better fight, who single hast maintained
Against revolted multitudes the cause
Of truth, in word mightier than they in arms,
And for the testimony of truth hast borne
Universal reproach, far worse to bear
Than violence; for this was all thy care—
To stand approved in sight of God, though worlds
Judged thee perverse.

VII

In this consideration of Milton I have emphasized the depth of his convictions, the intensity of his imagination, the magnificence and splendor of his diction. When we come to speak of Shakespeare, we need to emphasize his comprehensiveness, his objectivity, his universality. It is difficult at first to see how he can be summed up in any formula, and especially how he can be made to fit into any conception of the moral law or moral order. It is hazardous to say that Shakespeare believed anything, for he can never be identified with any of his various characters. If you interpret their sayings as his, you can prove anything; for he has created villains and criminals of every description, optimists, pessimists, cynics, and radiant and abundant personalities. One reason why he is so much more comprehensive than Milton or Bunyan is that he had a sense of humor and created not only his inimitable series of great comedies but the supreme character of Falstaff, who was not only witty in himself but the cause of wit in others. If ever a man saw life steadily and saw it whole, he did. He certainly would have been out of place if he had sought to live with the Puritans, but he would have understood them. It is difficult to think of him and Milton meeting at the Mermaid Tavern, or on the "Mayflower."

And yet I maintain that one may deduce rightly from his plays as a whole a very definite idea of moral order, of the struggle between the good and evil forces of the world. That is why Stuart Sherman in his volume *Contemporary Literature* wrote as his last chapter "Shakespeare: Our Contemporary." He makes out his case that, amid the confusion of the various voices in modern literature, many of them extremely realistic and deterministic, Shakespeare's distinction between good and evil values, his view of man as a total being—spiritual as well as physical and intellectual—his representation of both the comedy and tragedy of man's life, are all needed to counteract certain unhealthy tendencies in the modern drama and in naturalistic fiction.

It is still a much mooted question as to whether Shakespeare's sonnets are to be considered autobiographical. There are two of his sonnets that give monumental expression to the conception of a moral order : one drawing a distinction between the soul and the body, and the other summing up in a few suggestive lines various aspects of the wrongness of the world. The first has a note of asceticism and might have been written by a medieval poet; soul and body seem to be at war with each other :

> Poor soul, the centre of my sinful earth,
> [Thrall to] these rebel powers that thee array,
> Why dost thou pine within and suffer dearth,
> Painting thy outward walls so costly gay?
> Why so large cost, having so short a lease,
> Dost thou upon thy fading mansion spend?
> Shall worms, inheritors of this excess,
> Eat up thy charge? Is this thy body's end?
> Then, soul, live thou upon thy servant's loss,
> And let that pine to aggravate thy store;
> Buy terms divine in selling hours of dross;
> Within be fed, without be rich no more :
> So shalt thou feed on Death, that feeds on men,
> And Death once dead, there's no more dying then.

The other might have been written as the preface to his tragedies :

> Tir'd with all these, for restful death I cry,
> As, to behold desert a beggar born,
> And needy nothing trimm'd in jollity,
> And purest faith unhappily forsworn,
> And gilded honour shamefully misplac'd,
> And maiden virtue rudely strumpeted,
> And right perfection wrongfully disgrac'd,
> And strength by limping sway disabled,

And art made tongue-tied by authority,
And folly, doctor-like, controlling skill,
And simple truth miscall'd simplicity,
And captive good attending captain ill:
  Tir'd with all these, from these would I be gone,
  Save that, to die, I leave my love alone.

I leave out of consideration his comedies and his historical plays and concentrate attention upon his tragedies, which were written when he was at the height of his mastery of dramatic technique and when he revealed the heights and depths of his knowledge of human nature. It is generally agreed that he had passed through some sort of tragic disillusionment or suffering. Be that as it may, he shows that he understood everything in human nature that leads to defeat, suffering, and tragedy. Run over in your mind, if you will, the great series of tragedies which were written between 1600 and 1612. We find such an accumulation of folly, melancholy, murder, ambition, jealousy, lust, suffering, and death, such a seeming triumph of evil over good, such suggestions of the mystery of "all this unintelligible world," that we are overwhelmed. A deeper reading of these plays will convince any open-minded man that Shakespeare was always aware of what is bad and what is good, and that the evil characters always come to defeat and they know it. In other words, he gave abundant testimony to the fact that there is a moral order which cannot be violated without punishment here and now.

Hamlet's words to his mother, contrasting his father and the incestuous king—Hyperion and the satyr—put the whole difference between good and evil in a nutshell: "Look here, upon this picture, and on this." While the dramatist emphasizes certain evil forces such as witches and ghosts and to some extent the influence of heavenly bodies on human beings, they are not the primary sources of evil; they rather respond to what is going on in the minds of his characters. The cynical and wicked Edmund makes sport of the "excellent foppery of the world" that makes "guilty of our disasters the sun, the moon, and the stars, as if we were villains on necessity, fools by heavenly compulsion." Cassius reminds Brutus that it is

> not in our stars,
> But in ourselves, that we are underlings.

Nor does Shakespeare follow the Greeks in making destiny or fate the cause of man's misfortunes, notwithstanding Hamlet's famous saying that "there's a divinity that shapes our ends." In every case the source of the tragedy is either an environment that is hostile or a certain inner weakness or crime, or both. The moral order that we find in these plays demands perfection. Folly as in King Lear; a tendency to irresolution or to melancholy as in Hamlet; an over-romantic passion as in Romeo, Juliet, Antony, and Cleopatra; a pride that has no patience with the multitude as in Coriolanus; a credulousness or childlike submission to a cunning intellect as in Othello; a failure to understand the trend of events in the political world as in Brutus—all these lead to misfortune and tragedy as surely as crime, selfishness, greed, and other sins.

VIII

The play that best represents all these points and that has an especial meaning at the present time is *King Lear*. Here we have the suggestion of the cosmic nature of evil—the storm on the heath that breaks with pitiless power on the heads of Lear and his associates; the gods who seem at times to be in confederacy with evil; the animal passions into which men seem to descend when they manifest the qualities of the bear, the wolf, the fox; the criminal passions of Edmund, Regan, and Goneril—all these exist in the chaos and anarchy of a world turned upside down. Man reels back into the jungle. From a multitude of passages the following are typical:

> Ingratitude, thou marble-hearted fiend,
> More hideous when thou show'st thee in a child
> Than the sea-monster!

> You see me here, you gods, a poor old man,
> As full of grief as age; wretched in both!

> Blow, winds, and crack your cheeks! Rage! Blow!
> You cataracts and hurricanoes, spout
> Till you have drench'd our steeples, drown'd the cocks!
> You sulphurous and thought-executing fires,
> Vaunt-couriers of oak-cleaving thunderbolts,
> Singe my white head! And thou, all-shaking thunder,
> Strike flat the thick rotundity o' the world!
> Crack nature's moulds, all germens spill at once,
> That makes ingrateful man!

> Here I stand, your slave,
> A poor, infirm, weak, and despis'd old man;
> But yet I call you servile ministers,
> That will with two pernicious daughters join
> Your high-engender'd battles 'gainst a head
> So old and white as this.

> As flies to wanton boys, are we to the gods,
> They kill us for their sport.

And my poor fool is hang'd! No, no, no life!
Why should a dog, a horse, a rat, have life,
And thou no breath at all? Thou 'lt come no more,
Never, never, never, never, never!

Vex not his ghost; O let him pass! He hates him
That would upon the rack of this tough world
Stretch him out longer.

The oldest hath borne most; we that are young
Shall never see so much, nor live so long.

Never, I believe, has the power of evil been more strongly represented, and yet the final impression of the play is not that of rebellion. After all, the king has been purged by affliction—"Nothing almost sees miracles but misery." He has learned something of the darker side of human suffering—"Poor naked wretches, wheresoe'er you are." Cordelia shines like the stars after a stormy night and is beautiful in death—

> Upon such sacrifices, my Cordelia,
> The gods themselves throw incense.

Kent and Edgar stand out at the end, after all their loyal devotion ready to begin a new order and to inaugurate a new kingdom. Edmund, Regan, and Goneril know that all their plans and persecutions have been thwarted. Evil carries its own punishment, and good is its own reward. The tragedy is that in this conflict between good and evil forces the good seems wasted; it costs the moral order so much to throw out from itself the evil. The painful mystery of vicarious suffering constitutes the tragedy.

In his most illuminating book *Shakespearean Tragedy* F. H. Bradley briefly sums up what I am trying to say about the tragedies: "We remain confronted with the inexplicable fact, or the no less inexplicable appearance, of a world travailing for perfection, but bringing to birth, together with glorious good, an evil which it is able to overcome only by self-torture and self-waste." I think we may add to this statement that in these plays suffering is characteristic of great souls. We are not allowed to go further than this; "the rest is silence." Shakespeare has no suggestion of immortality or of the love of God. We must wait till Browning for any such hope and faith to illumine the darkness and mystery of human tragedy. But it means no little that the greatest dramatist of all time, and we like to think the greatest writer that ever lived, presents dramatically and not didactically the everlasting difference between good and evil.

This idea is more succinctly expressed in *Macbeth*. The gradual deterioration of a character who originally had great possibilities for good and the even more striking deterioration of Lady Macbeth are evident to all readers of the play. They have just enough good left in them to show remorse for their sins. Dr. W. C. Curry in two notable chapters in his *Shakespeare's Philosophical Patterns* has presented the demonic metaphysics which underlies the place of the witches in the drama and in the changing character of Macbeth. He says quite truly that the witches or weird sisters symbolize evil in its most malignant form, comparable to the influence of the fallen angels in Milton. They appeal to the human imagination and stir up passions, or, rather, reinforce passions. But they do not explain Macbeth's fall:

His will seems to be entirely untrammeled and his liberty of free choice absolute. . . . After the first crime, however, one cannot help observing that a change has taken place in the man. . . . It is . . . a profound alteration in the state of his personality, an astounding dislocation of the very center of being, which fixes itself immediately in a habit inclining to further crime. This change is progressive: while sin plucks on sin, the good in him seems to diminish, leaving his nature finally an almost completely barren waste of evil. . . . In proportion as the good in him diminishes, his liberty of free choice is determined more and more by evil inclination and . . . he cannot choose the better course. . . . In short, Macbeth's spiritual experience is a representation on the stage of the traditional Christian conception of a hunman soul on its way to the Devil. . . .

[At the end] his being has shrunk to such little measure that he has lost his former sensitiveness to good and evil; he has supped so full with horrors and the disposition of evil is so fixed in him that nothing can start him. His conscience is numbed so that he escapes the domination of fears. . . . In this universal negation he approaches the borderland of spiritual annihilation.[3]

IX

It is a striking fact that when the dramatist had finished his series of tragedies, he wrote what are called his romantic comedies, in which we have clearly the triumph of the good over the evil. *The Winter's Tale, Cymbeline,* and above all *The Tempest* start off with all the evidence of tragic forces in control, but all of them end in reconciliation, forgiveness, restoration, happiness. It is as if Shakespeare had said that after all good may be prosperous and successful, even in this world. This is where he contrasts with a writer like Thomas Hardy, who reveals in his novels and his poems only that which is dark and even morbid. Life's little and big ironies, time's laughingstocks, the play of the immortals with a character like Tess—all these suggest the single vision of the modern writer. Just as Shakespeare shows us in his early

[3] By permission of the publisher, Louisiana State University Press.

plays that life may take the form of innocent enjoyment, happy laughter, romantic love, sparkling humor; that there is a forest of Arden and the beautiful forest near Athens in which these characters have full reign; just as in his historical plays we have, along with the kings who are cruel or decadent, those like Henry V, who was his representation of England's ideal king, and whose words and phrases have rung through English history like the roll of Drake's drum; so in these later plays we have the triumph of joy over despair, of love over hatred, of life over death.

We like to think that his very last play was *The Tempest,* and that Prospero is Shakespeare himself at the end of his great creative period, in command of all the enemies who had sought to destroy him, of the forces in nature that challenge the inventiveness of man, the lord of a happy realm in which the magical melody of Ariel and the love of Miranda and Ferdinand irradiate the world. Even Caliban, a living embodiment of the grosser nature of man, a missing link between animal and man, feels that something has happened beyond his ken, and he turns from the drunken revelers whom he was ready to salute as gods to apprehend somewhat dimly the superior qualities of Prospero. When Prospero, forgiving those who had robbed him of his power, says that forgiveness is the rarer virtue, he has attained to something that approaches the spirit of the Christ.

CHAPTER III

PROPHETS AND SEERS

SARGENT'S frieze of the Hebrew prophets in the Boston Public Library, reproduced as it has been in many forms, used to be a familiar picture in many homes and especially in pastors' studies. The artist portrayed the faces of the leading prophets, most of them with shaggy beards and gaunt faces, and all of them with deep, penetrating eyes. These prophets from Amos to the great Prophet of the Exile constitute one of the most remarkable groups of men that ever lived on the earth. As interpreted by George Adam Smith, in their relation to their respective ages and with a suggestion of their significance for later ages, and especially for the modern period, their prophetic books have the quality of great literature and at the same time reveal some of the essential and fundamental ideas of religion. They constitute one of the indispensable manuals of applied religion and of enlightened citizenship.

And yet I know of no group of men who have been so often misinterpreted. The prophet in the minds of many is one who merely foretells events; he is a sort of magician who can predict places and names and exact dates, a sort of dummy who writes as if some superior god held his hand; he is a passive being, unrelated to his age and his people. Nothing could be wider of the mark. The prophets, different as they were in temperament and in environment, had certain common characteristics that distinguished them from the priests and the wise men or sages. Their appeals were different. The priest inherited the traditions and laws that came down from Mount Sinai. His appeal was: do good because it is the law, and avoid evil because it is contrary to the law. The wise man, who gave us what is called the wisdom literature, appealed to experience and common sense: do good because if you watch the ways of men and reflect thereon you will see that goodness or righteousness is justified as good sense and as wisdom; avoid evil because sin is folly.

Now the prophet spoke from his direct consciousness of God's voice within him—"The Lord God hath spoken, who can but prophesy?" He may, like Amos, have come from outside the temple, from the wilderness and the desert, and his efforts may have been directed against organized and institutional religion—the seventh chapter of Amos represents vividly this conflict between prophet and priest. Or, like Isaiah, he may have grown up in the temple, accustomed to its forms and ceremonies, but finding a new revelation of truth necessary which would modify or revolutionize institutions and forms. In either case he claimed to have a direct revelation from God, and he reinforced his own words by "Thus saith the Lord."

This consciousness of God's presence and voice was associated with a knowledge of his people and of the particular conditions that surrounded him. No sociologist of our time has attempted more earnestly and with more understanding to see into social and political conditions. Some of the prophets were statesmen who understood better than anybody else what was necessary to save the Hebrew people, and as their experience broadened and their vision was extended they saw the Hebrew people in relation to other peoples and races. The evolution of this increasing knowledge and vision through several centuries is one of the most interesting studies that can be made of the Bible. Whether we think of Isaiah literally wresting Jerusalem from what seemed the inevitable conquest by the Assyrians, or of the Prophet of the Exile bringing comfort to his people in Babylon and pointing out to them their future role as the suffering servants of Jehovah for all the people of the world, they must be reckoned among the great teachers and citizens of the world, who preserved the spirit of Judaism until it should be fulfilled in the revelation that came with the Messiah.

Some of them did foresee the coming of one greater than Moses or David or the prophets, but it is only honest to say that they saw him in different lights, some foretelling one who would bring political and material power to Israel—prophecies that Jesus himself had constantly to contend against in his own spiritual ideals. The fifty-third chapter of Isaiah anticipated the Messiah who would be the great sufferer for man. Because they knew the mind and heart of God and because they had a realistic sense of the unfolding of history, the prophets could thus foretell the coming of a larger and more spiritual religion. The astronomer can predict with absolute accuracy what will happen in the heavenly bodies thousands of years hence; so these prophets could write in such a way that we of today may find in their utterances the best interpretations of religion applied to whatever social, economic, and political conditions may arise. One vision they had that has never been fulfilled is universal peace, when men's spears shall be turned into pruninghooks.

II

So much needs to be said of the Hebrew prophets in order that we may find their successors in later periods of history.

It is an utter misrepresentation of God as a revealer of truth to say that inspiration ceased with the completion of the Bible. All through history the prophet and the seer have existed. What I wish to emphasize now is that the conditions that prevailed in England during the Victorian age called for men of this type, and that they were forthcoming in men who had the characteristics we have emphasized as belonging to the prophets. Carlyle and Ruskin might have been taken as models by Sargent when he made his immortal frieze. Carlyle came out of Scotland—a poor man with poverty as an inheritance, and with a rough accent which he hurled into the faces of the fashionable people who heard him lecture in London. He awoke and startled a constantly increasing reading public. Ruskin, born to the purple from the standpoint both of wealth and of culture, changed in the middle years of his life from an interpreter of art and beauty to a prophet of righteousness and justice. They reflected in their own idioms the most characteristic utterances of the Hebrew prophets: "Woe to them that are at ease in Zion!" and, "What doth the Lord require of thee, but to do justly, and to love mercy, and to walk humbly with thy God?" Likewise in America, where conditions were much the same as in England, men like Emerson and Walt Whitman—seers rather than prophets—in very different ways attacked conventional ideas and institutions and upheld the ideals that were born out of their own experience and a new environment.

The Victorian age, with its industrial prosperity, its amazing mechanical devices, and its shibboleth of freedom and democracy which seemed to have solved all man's problems, was a fitting background for such men. One of the culminating points in the age was the exhibition of 1851, when there were displayed at the Crystal Palace in London all the products of the civilized world, and especially the evidences in England and throughout the empire of the great progress made in applied science. It was the aim of the Prince Consort, who brought to the task all of his German thoroughness, his great power of organization, and his devotion to the England which he had come to think of, at last, as his own country, to show the nation that in the lucrative arts of peace rather than in the destructive panoply of war lay their moral and material salvation. Macaulay spoke of it as a singularly happy year, "of peace, plenty, good feeling, innocent pleasure, and national glory of the best and surest sort."

This exhibition was but one of many stages in the marvelous increase in the wealth and commerce of England. Tennyson voiced the hopes of that time when he wrote of the visions of his youth in "Locksley Hall," forecasting even the coming of the airplane. Macaulay, the exact opposite of the prophetic type, expressed in terms of philosophy and ethics the significance of this material progress. His essay on "Lord Bacon" is fundamental reading for one who would understand the dominant spirit of a middle-class England moving by leaps and bounds in its mastery of the external forces of the world. His comparison of Plato and Bacon, one-sided and narrow as it is, is an exposition of the difference between an idealistic philosophy and a practical, utilitarian philosophy. Contrasting their attitude to arithmetic, geometry, astronomy, and medicine, he leads up to a sweeping generalization:

To make men perfect was no part of Bacon's plan. His humble end was to make imperfect men comfortable. . . .

The aim of the Platonic philosophy was to exalt man into a god. The aim of the Baconian philosophy was to provide man with what he requires while he continues to be man. The aim of the Platonic philisophy was to raise us far above vulgar wants. The aim of the Baconian philosophy was to supply our vulgar wants. The former aim was noble; but the latter was attainable. . . .

An acre in Middlesex is better than a principality in Utopia. The smallest actual good is better than the most magnificent promises of impossibilities. The wise man of the Stoics would, no doubt, be a grander object than a steam-engine. But there are steam-engines. And the wise man of the Stoics is yet to be born.

Comparing the two philosophies by the test of "profitable truth" he speaks for the new philosophy words that are like a paean of praise for modern material civilization; some of it sounds strikingly ironic in view of conditions in the world today when applied science like a Frankenstein has created a veritable monster of destruction:

It has lengthened life; it has mitigated pain; it has extinguished disease; it has increased the fertility of the soil; it has given new securities to the mariner; it has furnished new arms to the warrior; . . . it has guided the thunderbolt innocuously from heaven to earth; it has lighted up the night with the splendour of the day; it has extended the range of the human vision; . . . it has annihilated distance; . . . it has enabled man to descend to the depths of the sea, to soar into the air, to penetrate securely into the noxious recesses of the earth. . . . There are but a part of its fruits, and of its first fruits. For it is a philosophy which never rests, which has never attained, which is never perfect. Its law is progress, A point which yesterday was invisible is its goal to-day, and will be its starting-post to-morrow.

It was on the basis of such exuberant complacency and optimism that the ethics or philosophy of utility and progress, characteristic of both England and America, was accepted. Bentham and the Mills were all confident that in industrialism and democracy the key to the world's salvation had been found. But the great majority of Victorian writers were quick to detect the fallacy of this facile optimism. Even the radiant visions of Tennyson in "Locksley Hall" faded in the poet's mind before the conditions that he realized and expressed in *Maud* and still more in "Locksley Hall Sixty Years After." Carlyle in his *Chartism* and *Past and Present* saw underneath the brilliant surface of English industrial prosperity the volcanic fires of hunger, disease, and poverty. Arthur Hugh Clough in "The Latest Decalogue" treated the whole effect of modern materialism on morality and religion with sarcasm and irony; while Mrs. Browning, with a vigor of sentiment not always characteristic of her, lashed out in "The Cry of the Children" at those who made capital out of children working in the factories. The Pre-Raphaelite artists and poets rebelled in terms of beauty against the ugliness and sordidness of an industrial civilization. William Morris, especially by his handmade furniture and his beautiful medieval printing, had a large influence in producing by hand the things which had come to be made by machine. Mass production on a large scale seemed to do away with the necessity for the arts and crafts movement, but in out-of-the-way corners artists and architects did what they could to stem the tide.

III

Ruskin, midway of his life, turned from the criticism of art to the criticism of an industrial society. It was not a sudden revolution in his way of thinking, for he had gradually come to see that there could be no great national art without a national faith that went beyond the range of utilitarianism and mechanism. If one reads the first lecture, on "Kings' Treasuries," in *Sesame and Lilies,* he finds the author breaking away from his reflections on literature to a general condemnation of a people who cannot appreciate literature because, as he says, they have despised nature, art, science, beauty in all its forms, and compassion. So he turned from *Modern Painters* and *Stones of Venice* to *Unto This Last, The Crown of Wild Olive,* and *Fors Clavigera.* He did not simply write about the conditions of the poor and their exclusion from all that constitutes a happy life—pure air, pure water, pure earth, and the immaterial things, admiration, hope, and love—but he spent his inherited fortune in trying to alleviate their lot and to bring them into the kingdom of social justice and freedom. His scheme for reviving the medieval guild was fantastic; his desire to abolish all forms of industry and to return to medieval society was fanciful; but his protest against social injustice, selfishness, and ugliness has been one of the primary influences in awakening men to the dangers of a mechanical world. Comparing the deities of the age of Pericles, "Wisdom," and of medieval faith, "Comfort," and of the Renaissance, "Pleasure," he invented as the appropriate deity for modern England the "Goddess of Getting-on" or "Britannia of the Market," to whom are built not great cathedrals but "railroad mounds, vaster than the walls of Babylon; . . . railroad stations, vaster than the temple of Ephesus," and exchanges where money is lord of all.

Ruskin realized the commercial spirit of the age, the materialism that was dwarfing the souls of men. The grinding habits of the industrial world pressed heavily upon his spirit;

the lack of justice and human sympathy touched him until he could no longer be silent. Instead of an interpreter in the House Beautiful he became a preacher of righteousness. In book after book and lecture after lecture he cried out against modern conditions with an emphasis that reminds one of the Hebrew prophets—his voice growing more and more intense, and his heart more deeply stirred, until nature could stand no further strain and gave way.

One may appreciate the difference between Ruskin's earlier and later life by contrasting two portraits of him. One is the face of a well-bred, cultured man, accustomed from his youth to all the privileges that wealth can afford—travel, art, literature. There is a look of serenity in his eyes and repose on his brow. The other has the long flowing hair and shaggy beard of one of Sargent's prophets; large, luminous eyes, with an intense glow, look out from under a frowning brow. In his younger years he was the friend of artists, among whom were Millais, Rossetti, and Holman Hunt; in later life he became identified in the public mind with Maurice, Carlyle, Kingsley, William Booth, and Tolstoy—all of whom heard the voice of the Lord, although each responded thereto in his own characteristic manner. In framing an ideal of life these men were, however, narrow, ascetic, rude, as compared with the wider and more refined culture of Ruskin. There was not such a change in his life as in the case of Tolstoy or Carlyle. He still believed in beauty.

In his youth he built his Palace of Art—as did the soul in Tennyson's poem of that name—far above the confusion and turmoil of the world, with splendid courts and cloisters and fountains without and tapestries and paintings within, and there he lived in the enjoyment of all the soul might crave; but by 1860 shadows had come to vex the calm soul—shadows of suffering men and women—and murmurs of discontent from the valley below disturbed his rest. His first impulse was to tear down his palace; but no! he will leave it, and someday he will bring back from the valley his toiling brethren to enjoy with him the highest privileges of earth's more favored sons.

It is evident, from all that has been said, that Ruskin placed the emphasis of his message after 1860 on social and industrial conditions. He says many good things in *Sesame and Lilies* and *The Crown of Wild Olive,* and in other books, about ideals of culture and the problems of modern life, but that which weighed most heavily upon him was the unequal opportunities and privileges of men. The man in the factory, on the farm, in the sweat shop; the man in crowded and unhealthy tenement houses; the man who has not "pure air, water, and earth"; the man into whose life comes no "admiration, hope, and love," no beautiful things to make him happy—this man was the subject of his thought and the burden of his heart. In the introductory letter of *Fors Clavigera* he says, by way of dedication to his new calling:

For my own part, I will put up with this state of things, passively, not an hour longer. I am not an unselfish person, nor an Evangelical one; I have no particular pleasure in doing good; neither do I dislike doing it so much as to expect to be rewarded for it in another world. But I simply cannot paint, nor read, nor look at minerals, nor do anything else that I like, and the very light of the morning sky, when there is any—which is seldom, nowadays, near London—has become hateful to me, because of the misery that I know of, and see signs of, where I know it not, which no imagination can interpret too bitterly.

Therefore, as I have said, I will endure it no longer quietly;

82

but henceforward with any few or many who will help, do my poor best to abate this misery.

It is easy enough to laugh at Ruskin and call him a "dreamer," but the same epithet has been applied to every man who in his century dealt with the industrial problem. Many of Ruskin's ideas are crude and impracticable; some of his plans and schemes show a lack of proper sanity and judgment that should characterize a great reformer. His effort to create St. George's Guild, modeled on the medieval guilds and having many of the features of feudalism, excites merriment among the wise and the foolish, although we may well wish for the day to come when such vows might be taken and such promises kept. But after all has been said, after admitting that Ruskin's style suffered much from his violent philanthropy, that there is a strange mixture of conservatism and radicalism in his theories, that he seems to have had but little ability to put into operation the schemes he so fondly contemplated—yes, after all this, we are constrained to believe that there are things in these writings that mankind will not willingly let die. They may not offer a satisfactory solution of the industrial problem, but they have given, and will give, an impulse to the more serious consideration of such problems; and many principles he laid down will be the working basis of "that great race which is to be." We do not hear as much of the "economic man" as we used to, nor of the law of supply and demand.

It is no wonder that workingmen all over England consider many of Ruskin's works, notably *Fors Clavigera* and *Unto This Last,* as among the prime necessities of life. They know that he was in sympathy with them, that he gave his money—nay more, his life—to the advancement of their interests. He insisted in all his works that "the manufacture of souls of good quality is worthy of our best attention," that "there is no wealth but life." He struck forcefully at many of the evils of commercialism, speaking of treasures "heavy with human tears" and money "accumulated at the cost of life or by limitations of it; that is to say, either by hastening the deaths of men or preventing their births." He declared: "The aim of political economy is the multiplication of human life at the highest standard. The consummation of all wealth is the producing as many as possible full-breathed, bright-eyed, and happy-hearted human creatures." Now and then, as in "The Mystery of Life and Its Arts," he brought before his readers, as in a flash, the suffering of men and women and the responsibility of society: "As long as there are any who have no blankets for their beds, and no rags for their bodies, so long it is blanket-making and tailoring we must set people to work at—not lace."

Such convictions as these made Ruskin unhappy, and caused the world to indulge in much abuse and ridicule at his expense. He became a "hermit and heretic." For a while he wrote with great power—"thoughts that breathe and words that burn"—but after 1878 he wrote nothing of any considerable importance. His old age was not one of healthy activity, as was that of Tennyson, who after writing for sixty years closed his poetic career with one of the most beautiful of all his lyrics; or of Browning, who grew old like his own Rabbi, and in the last month of his life wrote his most hopeful and, in many respects, strongest poem. Nor was his old age one of repose like that of Wordsworth, who wrote in 1818 his last great poem, but lived on in peace and serenity till 1850. Ruskin's last years were stormy like those of Landor, and bitter like those of Carlyle. He lived at

Brantwood, on Lake Coniston—"among woods and hills and pure breezes"—with Titians and Turners in the rooms of the classic-looking place. His last years were not crowned with peace, as would have befitted one whose thoughts had always dwelt on high themes, and whose mind was a "mansion for all lovely forms"; but the "Storm Cloud," of which he had spoken so eloquently to the English people, settled down upon him. His mind was touched with infirmity. His voice, once so musical, became harsh and discordant. Partly by reason of his own physical and mental constitution, and partly because the time was out of joint, his last years added nothing to his fame as a writer nor to his peace of mind and nobility of character.

IV

Carlyle is an even better illustration of the prophet's temperament and message. He was terribly in earnest and often violent in his denunciations of a complacent society. The three central chapters of the second book of *Sartor Resartus,* which ought to be read first, constitute the story of his progress from disillusionment, doubt, and absolute despair to a hard-won faith based upon courage, defiance, and militant idealism.

The "Everlasting No" is his synonym for skepticism as to all the values of life; the phrase represents what others have expressed in Mephistopheles, the spirit that denies, or Satan, or the popular devil. It is that in man's inner life and in the constitution of things, the cosmos, which says No to all his hopes and aspirations. To Carlyle this power had expressed itself in the negative side of the clothes philosophy, hereafter to be explained, in a grim humor which saw through the shams of the world, and in a rationalism which left no room for hope or faith. Some sentences and phrases represent different phases of this period in his life:

My Loadstars were blotted out; in that canopy of grim fire shone no star.

... a hot fever of anarchy and misery raving within.

Is there no God, then; but at best an absentee God, sitting idle, ever since the first Sabbath, at the outside of his Universe, and *seeing* it go?

... shouting question after question into the Sibyl-cave of Destiny, and receiving no Answer but an Echo.

The universe was ... one huge, dead, immeasurable Steam-engine, rolling on, in its dead indifference, to grind me limb from limb.

That he was able to triumph over all these obstacles was due to a certain spirit of defiance and righteous indignation that is expressed in the last three paragraphs of the chapter:

... and I asked myself "What *art* thou afraid of? Wherefore, like a coward, dost thou for ever pip and whimper, and go cowering and trembling? Despicable biped! What is the sum-total of the worst that lies before thee? Death? Well, Death; and say the pangs of Tophet too, and all that the Devil and Man may, will, or can do against thee! Hast thou not a heart; canst thou not suffer whatso it be; and, as a Child of Freedom, though outcast, trample Tophet itself under thy feet, while it consumes thee? Let it come, then; I will meet it and defy it!" And as I so thought, there rushed like a stream of fire over my whole soul; and I shook base Fear away from me for ever. I was strong, of unknown strength; a spirit, almost a god. Ever from that time, the temper of my misery was changed: not

Fear or whining Sorrow was it, but Indignation and grim fire-eyed Defiance.

Thus had the EVERLASTING NO (*das ewige Nein*) pealed authorititatively through all the recesses of my Being, of my ME; and then was it that my whole ME stood up, in native God-created majesty, and with emphasis recorded its Protest. Such a Protest, the most important transaction in Life, may that same Indignation and Defiance, in a psychological point of view, be fitly called. The Everlasting No had said: "Behold, thou art fatherless, outcast, and the Universe is mine (the Devil's);" to which my whole ME now made answer: "*I* am not thine, but Free, and forever hate thee!"

It is from this hour that I incline to date my Spiritual New-birth, or Baphometic Fire-baptism; perhaps I directly there-upon began to be a Man.

The chapter entitled "The Everlasting Yea" represents the victorious outcome of this struggle, a changing from merely negative protests to a positive and creative faith. Carlyle means by the phrase that in the deepest soul of man and in the heart of the universe there is something which says Yea to man's hopes and aspirations. Such sentences as the following are expressions of this unconquerable faith:

The Universe is not dead and demoniacal, a charnel-house with spectres; but godlike, and my Father's!

What is nature? . . . Art thou not the "Living Garment of God?"

Love not Pleasure; love God. This is the EVERLASTANG YEA, wherein all contradiction is solved.

Doubt of any sort cannot be removed except by Action.

Believing, then, in the divineness of nature, the fatherhood of God, the brotherhood of men, the eternal verities of duty and self-renunciation, he comes to the conclusion of the whole matter by finding joy in creative work:

But it is with man's Soul as it was with Nature: the beginning of Creation is—Light. Till eye have vision, the whole members are in bonds. Divine moment, when over the tempest-tost Soul, as once over the wild-weltering Chaos, it is spoken: Let there be Light! Ever to the greatest that has felt such moment, is it not miraculous and God-announcing; even as, under simpler figures, to the simplest and least. The mad primeval Discord is hushed; the rudely-jumbled conflicting elements bind themselves into separate Firmaments: deep silent rock-foundations are built beneath; and the skyey vault with its everlasting Luminaries above: instead of a dark wasteful Chaos, we have a blooming, fertile, heaven-encompassed World.

I too could now say to myself: Be no longer a Chaos, but a World, or even Worldkin. Produce! Produce! Were it but the pitifulest infinitesimal fraction of a Product, produce it in God's name! 'Tis the utmost thou hast in thee; out with it, then. Up, up! Whatsoever thy hand findeth to do, do it with thy whole might. Work while it is called To-day, for the Night cometh, wherein no man can work.

Sartor Resartus is not easy reading; it demands most careful attention and study. The symbol of clothes, which Carlyle used to express his fundamental philosophy, has two aspects. Everything has an inner reality and an outward garment. If the inner reality is less than the outward form, there is the basis of satire or cynicism. If the inner reality is greater than the outward form or garment, we have the basis of idealism, or transcendentalism. Throughout the book

Carlyle is constantly exposing the shams that obscure reality. From one standpoint man is a "two-legged animal without feathers," a "miserable biped." From another he is a spirit, an "unutterable Mystery of Mysteries." One view issues in a philosophy of descendentalism, the philosophy of Swift, Mephistopheles, Voltaire; the other issues in transcendentalism, the characteristic philosophy of the great Germans. One is largely destructive, negative, and leads to the exposure of the false; the other is largely constructive, affirmative, and a revelation of the truth. Both are methods of seeing the truth, and both are necessary to complete and perfect vision. Never did a prophet invent a figurative language more adequate for the expression of truth.

There are times when the figure of clothes is lost sight of, but it is surprising how many illustrations are given in this book of the difference between what appears and what really is. Words may conceal thought because they are not things; language is the garment of thought and either fails to convey thought or suggests something that rises beyond the power of expression. Think of what a large part clothes play in history, and of how a museum in which the clothes of other generations are displayed may be the key to understanding history. Think of the outward robes and insignia of a king or a bishop which may or may not be the revelation of the man, or of the uniforms of the navy and the army, or of black shirts and red shirts, the Pope's tiara, the bishop's shovel hat, academic costume, which may be either absurd or the suggestion of something greater that lies behind them. Carlyle imagines in Book I, Chapter 9, what would happen if at a big ball of diplomats, dukes, bishops, generals, and the anointed Presence itself the clothes should suddenly fly off and reveal them as they are. Rarely has a writer displayed such a combination of humor and idealism.

Clothes also suggest the use of symbols, forms, conventions, institutions, organizations, ceremonies, formulae—all of which illustrate the two phases of the clothes philosophy. Any one of these may be less than the spirit that it is supposed to represent, or it may be more. The outstanding chapters are: "The World in Clothes," "The World out of Clothes," "Pure Reason," "Church-Clothes," "Symbols," "The Phoenix," "Old Clothes," "Organic Filaments," "The Dandiacal Body" (the whole social and industrial problem summed up in the contrast between the Dandy and the Drudge and the clothes they wear), and above all "Natural Supernaturalism," in which all history passes before Carlyle's perspective, and all nature and all men now living.

Generation after generation takes to itself the Form of a Body. . . . And then the Heaven-sent is recalled; his earthly Vesture falls away, and soon even to Sense becomes a Vanished Shadow. . . . Sense knows not; Faith knows not; only that it is through Mystery to Mystery, from God to God.

> *"We are such stuff*
> *As Dreams are made of."*

V

Carlyle's prophetic treatment of political and social questions grew out of the spiritual struggle just described, but his interest in workingmen was marked from the beginning. Son of a Scotch mason and carpenter, he inherited a deep sympathy for laborers of all types. His home was that of a peasant. One of his earliest recollections was hearing his father tell of Scotch laborers, in a time of famine, drinking water because they had no food. His father believed that the lot of the poor man was growing worse, that "something vicious was at the bottom of English and Scottish society, and that revolution in some form or other lay visibly ahead." In 1819, when Carlyle was passing through the spiritual crisis recorded in *Sartor Resartus,* his conversations with Edward Irving turned constantly upon the great uprising of the masses in Glasgow, Edinburgh, and Manchester. It was not, however, until 1829 that he gave expression to his political views in the essay entitled "Signs of the Times," the dominant idea of which is that in all respects his was a mechanical age, and in no respect more so than in its insistence that institutions—"mere political arrangements"—are the most important consideration. According to this theory our happiness depends entirely upon external circumstances—upon physical, practical, economic conditions as regulated by public laws. Men are to be guided only by their selfish interests. To both parties government is "emphatically a machine; to the discontented, a taxing machine; to the contented, a machine for securing property." The current political ideas were taken from the writings of Jeremy Bentham, who believed that his theory of "the greatest happiness of the greatest number" was to make a heaven of earth. As opposed to this mechanical view of government and society Carlyle insisted upon "Dynamics, which has to do with the inward, primary powers of man." Religion alone, which includes wonder and inspiration and direct vision, may be found the basis for a faith in a new and brighter era.

The following year Carlyle wrote *Sartor Resartus.* While the interest of the book centers largely about the spiritual crisis through which he passed, there are passages that bear upon the social and political problems of his time. Diogenes Teufelsdröckh—the German scholar created by the author as a medium for the expression of his own ideas—drinks a toast to "The Cause of the Poor in Heaven's Name," and indulges in remarks that show his leaning toward radical opinions. Side by side with his "high, silent, meditative Transcendentalism" is a practical tendency, at most political, toward "a certain prospective, and for the present quite speculative, Radicalism." The Philosophy of Clothes enunciated by him naturally includes a consideration of "Sansculottism," Carlyle's word for the uprising of the masses or men "without clothes" to wear. In speaking of the rugged, weather-tanned face of the toil-worn craftsman, whose back is bent and whose straight limbs and fingers are deformed in the service of man, he laments above all that "the light of his soul should go out; that no ray of heavenly or even of earthly knowledge should visit him; that his soul should lie blinded, dwarfed, stupefied, almost annihilated." In the chapter on "The Dandiacal Body" we have the sect of Drudges— "White Negroes," whose costumes, monastic vows of poverty and obedience, dark dwellings in cellars, and coarse food are sketched with all of Carlyle's satire and indignation. In contrast with these he draws the aristocrats, whose chief pastime is "preserving their game," and whose articles of faith, fashionable clothes, and idle talk are held up to the scorn of the reader. These two classes, hourly increasing, will one day part England between them. Dandyism and Drudgism are alike suspended over a thin crust or rind of the earth from which volcanic eruptions must deluge the world. They are like two opposite poles or batteries that may shiver the earth into impalpable smoke.

Carlyle in 1833 wrote in a letter a realistic picture of

"children working in Lancashire factories, laboring for sixteen hours a day, inhaling at every breath a quantity of cotton fuzz, falling asleep over their wheels, and roused again by the lash of thongs on their backs. . . . One pauses with a kind of amazed horror, to ask if this be earth, the place of Hope, or Tophet, where Hope never comes."

These words might well have been taken from Carlyle's *French Revolution,* which appeared in 1837. The central point of view from which this historical drama is written is that of the uprising of the masses of French peasants against the established order of the old feudal government and society. Through its vivid lines peer the faces of the hunger-stricken multitudes, "prowling through all the highways and by-ways of French existence." "Emptiness of pocket, of stomach, of head, and of heart," the ferocity of strength grounded on hunger, finally aroused these "uncomforted, untaught, and unfed" multitudes. If the scene shifts from the country to Paris, we have "in squalid garrets on Monday morning maternity awaking to hear children weeping for bread."

The cause of this suffering and of the revolution is found in the selfishness, the heartlessness, the hypocrisy, of the monarchy, the aristocracy, and the church. The old order must fall because it no longer fulfills the ideal for which it was created. It is the judgment of God upon the French people; it is "truth clad in hell-fire"; the nation had forgotten God. There are forces in the universe, terrible as the thunders of Sinai, and all nations in all ages are under the same dispensation. No philosophisms or encyclopedisms, shining in the glittering salons of Paris, could take the place of fundamental religion. No rose-pink vapor of sentimentalism, philanthropy, and feast of morals could be a substitute for strong and effective government; nor could democracy, whirlwindlike enveloping the world, control a revolution which must work itself out in fury and rage.

VI

In *Past and Present* is found the largest body of Carlyle's criticism of social conditions in Victorian England. Written a hundred years ago, it sounds as if written yesterday, although conditions have improved. It is one of the best illustrations of the contemporary value of a great classic.

In striking contrast with medieval life, which is portrayed in the second book, is the mechanical, atomic, individualistic structure of the modern era. Carlyle's presentation of the various classes in England is picturesque and vivid, even if exaggerated. The sovereign has become only a phantom. The aristocracy is composed for the most part of "Denizens of Mayfair" and "rosy fox-hunting" squires. They are the master unworkers, "pausing amidst their game preserves." In their social life they are dandies; in their intellectual and artistic life they are dilettanti; in their political activity they are "Donothings," "handsomely consuming the rents of England." Their speech is pungent, witty, ornamental, epigrammatic, but insincere in its cant and hypocrisy. They are, in a word, "a High Class without duties to do," owning the land but unwilling to assume the responsibility that ownership implies. Their epic might be called "Shirt-frills and the Man." At their worst they are like the apes by the Dead Sea in the Moslem legend—enchanted dilettanti who lost their souls because they would not listen to Moses.

As the aristocrats no longer govern, the priests no longer guide the nation in spiritual truth. Whether Carlyle considers the "stage-machinery," judiciously arranged, of modern Catholicism, the "wax-candles, organ-blasts, Gregorian chants, mass-brayings," and the pope, "the greatest Play-actor that at present draws salary in this world"; or the High Church movement of Pusey, Keble, and others with their emphasis upon the Thirty-nine Articles and the traditional faith; or Methodism, *"Egoism,* stretched out into the In-finite," and other forms of evangelical religion with their morbid introspection and ideas of individual salvation as contrasted with ideas of social regeneration—whichever form of Christianity he considers, he finds the same lack of original and creative faith. The popular theology had sur-rendered to the attacks made upon it by the rationalists of the eighteenth century and had adopted an intellectual com-promise which was little different in its effects from the "redtape" philosophy of the radicals and utilitariams of the day. There is only a dreamy cant with a "reminiscence of things noble and divine." The nation had forgotten God.

The really powerful man of the modern world, according to Carlyle, is the Captain of Industry. The one substantial fact standing out in the life and thought of two centuries is the marvelous achievement of inventors and manufacturers. Their epic is that of "Tools and the Man," and it is written not in words but in deeds that are world-wide in their in-fluence. But the industrial leader is under the dominion of Mammon. He is devoured by "naked Egoism, vulturous Greediness"; in his lust for gold he has given new meaning to the fable of Midas. He is the rich master worker, whose only hell is that of not succeeding. The "Millocracy" has in the counting houses and in Parliament taken the place of the aristocracy. Plugson of Undershot is not a whit better than the Choctaws and buccaneers of a vanished age. He is the resultant of the dominant economic laws of the "classic school" of economists and the champion of individualistic democracy.

So much for the shepherds, and now what of the sheep? The masses of workmen present a pitiable spectacle. Never, says Carlyle, was the lot of these same dumb millions of toilers so entirely unbearable as now. Two million sit in workhouses, poor-law prisons, their hopes and outlooks shut in by narrow walls. Whether we consider the brutal savages among the degraded Irish or the unemployed masses in England itself, we are impressed by the fatal paralysis of English industry. "We have more riches than any nation; we have less good than any other nation." The Manchester Insurrection, though put down by the power of the law, has put the question squarely to the nation, and the answer must be found, or the Sphinx of eternal destiny will devour us. The laborers do not object to hard work, but it is their lot "to live miserable, we know not why; to work sore and yet gain nothing; to be heart-worn, weary, yet isolated, unrelated, girt-in with a cold universal Laissez-faire: it is to die slowly all our life long, imprisoned in a deaf, dead, Infinite Injustice, as in the accursed iron belly of a Phalaris' Bull!" If it be answered that the lot of the poor has always been bad, it should be said that there are supportable and insupportable approximations to justice and right.

This, then, is Carlyle's indictment of the England of his day. Like Amos he smote and smote hard. He brought to bear every weapon of humor and righteous indignation to wake England up. The impression of the casual reader may be that he was a croaker, a destructive critic, a Jeremiah. As a matter of fact he treated every one of these classes of England as capable of changing entirely their habits of thought and their practices. Such aristocrats as the Earl of

Shaftesbury (Lord Ashley) or the Duke of Weimar pointed the way to the greatest service, and to the creation of a new aristocracy to whom the post of honor would be the post of difficulty, and whose noble crown would be a crown of thorns. So far from advocating the abolition of the church or underestimating the possibilities of the preacher or the priest, he would have them "find the point again," speak the right word, interpret religion in terms of social life. The church had only to modernize the words of the Hebrew prophet to become once more a source of power. It must stand for eternal justice as opposed to momentary expediency. Injustice has one enemy, the Almighty. Religion is the first and the last thing.

Carlyle's most original plea, however, was to the captains of industry to organize the chaos of modern industrial society. Casting behind them the profit-and-loss philosophy, the cash-payment theory of the relationship between labor and capital, and the law of supply and demand as the natural law of the economic world, let them become the noble master workers among the noble workers. The task of organizing labor would be a difficult one, but the very difficulty was a challenge. Such men as Prudence, the Quaker, with his contented workers about him pointed the way to the future. A true Chivalry of Labor might arise.

As the book progresses one can see that Carlyle becomes more and more committed to a program in which the state is to have greater authority and power. Social organization cannot be left to the caprice of any individual or class, however powerful or willing to do the right things.

"But," says someone, "you tell us the evil and do not tell us how it is to be cured." Is not democracy the cure for all the ills pointed out here? Carlyle maintains that democracy, *as then understood and practiced,* does not solve the problem. It lays the emphasis on individual liberty, which for the working millions may be "a liberty to die by want of food," or "a still more fatal liberty to live in want of work." Liberty may be the worst condition for men who are slaves to their passions and need above all guidance and direction. Political liberty, or the right of suffrage, may mean nothing when not associated with industrial liberty. Furthermore, the demagogue is the natural product of democratic institutions —a Sir Jabesh Windbag, "weak in the faith of a God . . .; strong only in the faith that Paragraphs and Plausibilities bring votes; that Force of Public Opinion, as he calls it, is the primal Necessity of Things, and highest God we have." When to the power of the demagogue in our "National Palaver"—Carlyle's name for Parliament—is added the power of money in bribing voters, we have "Mammonism preying on the vitals of Society." The aristocracy, which has been in the habit of governing England, seeks to throttle the power of capital, the only effective force in our modern world, while the strong capitalistic party cries, "Hands off!" in the fierce competition of business. And all of these facts result in a condition where government is negative rather than a directing force—"Anarchy plus a Constable." Democracy breaks down in the fundamental demands of government—it is inefficient.

In only one respect is modern government successful, and that is in the making of an army. Out of "ragged losels, runaway apprentices, starved weavers, thieving valets, an entirely broken population" is made a well-organized body of men preparing for the defense of the country. That one fact is prophecy of what government might do in the organization of an army against starvation, chaos, stupidity. The function of government must be extended to include measures of sanitation, employment of the unemployed, the education of the masses, emigration to the less crowded places of the world, shorter hours of labor, better conditions under which men may work, and many other needs of modern society. The teaching of agriculture, the inspection of mines, the organizing of profit-sharing industries, might well be included in the sphere of its operations. If democracy can organize these forces in an efficient way, then let it cease to be a negative thing and become an aggressive, organizing force. If it cannot, then it must give way to some other form of government where the best and wisest and strongest men will rule.

This last analysis is the key to the whole matter. Carlyle was right in his criticism of democracy as then understood, but most men who believe in universal suffrage would insist that the gradual acquisition of this right by the successive extensions of democracy was the only way to bring about the state which Carlyle visualized. Democracy in America has often failed to secure the best leaders—the "heroes" that figured so largely in Carlyle's imagination—but more recently great leaders in both England and America have done much to organize the state in terms of a larger social consciousness. It is given to no men to see all the phases of a complex subject, but Carlyle saw many of them, and there is no better evidence of his insight and prophetic power than *Past and Present*.

No better statement has been made of the permanent value of Carlyle's writings on social subjects than that by John Morley in a singularly discriminating and illuminating essay. Incidentally, it defines the work of the prophet in all ages:

One of Mr. Carlyle's chief and just glories is, that for more than forty years he has clearly seen, and kept constantly and conspicuously in his own sight and that of his readers, the profoundly important crisis in the midst of which we are living. The moral and social dissolution in progress about us, and the enormous peril of sailing blindfold and haphazard, without rudder or compass or chart, have always been fully visible to him, and it is no fault of his if they have not become equally plain to his contemporaries. The policy of drifting has had no countenance from him. That a society should be likely to last with hollow and scanty faith, with no government, with a number of institutions hardly one of them real, with a horrible mass of poverty-stricken and hopeless subjects . . . he has boldly and often declared to be . . . incredible. . . . What seems to many of us the extreme inefficiency or worse of his solutions, still allows us to feel grateful for the vigour and perspicacity with which he has pressed on the world the urgency of the problem.

VII

The best contemporary criticism of *Past and Present* was written by Emerson in the *Dial,* and the first edition of *Sartor Resartus* was published in Boston under the supervision and patronage of Emerson. Even on the basis of some of Carlyle's earlier essays, Emerson had sought him out in the wilderness of Craigenputtock and had told him that he had come from the ends of the earth to greet him as a new prophet in the world. Never were two men more unlike in physical appearance, in temperament, or in style. Emerson had a benignant smile, a serene countenance, a gentle voice, a smooth diction punctured with dynamic epigrams. One would have little suspected, as he began to read his address to the Phi Beta Kappa Society of Harvard in 1837, that a new prophet had arisen. Holmes and Lowell both left accounts of the effect on the audience of this "declaration of independence of American letters," but from beginning to end it was charged with almost revolutionary thought. After a few conventional references to the society and to the celebration of the annual festival, he boldly announced a new era:

Thus far, our holiday has been simply a friendly sign of the survival of the love of letters amongst a people too busy to give to letters any more. As such it is precious as the sign of an indestructible instinct. Perhaps the time is already come when it ought to be, and will be, something else; when the sluggard intellect of this continent will look from under its iron lids and fill the postponed expectation of the world with something better than the exertions of mechanical skill. Our day of dependence, our long apprenticeship to the learning of other lands, draws to a close. The millions that around us are rushing into life, cannot always be fed on the sere remains of foreign harvests. Events, actions arise, that must be sung, that will sing themselves. Who can doubt that poetry will revive and lead in a new age, as the star in the constellation Harp, which now flames in our zenith, astronomers announce, shall one day be the polestar for a thousand years?

After discussing nature, books, and life or experience as the basis of independent thought and action, he concluded:

This confidence in the unsearched might of man belongs, by all motives, by all prophecy, by all preparation, to the American Scholar. We have listened too long to the courtly muses of Europe. The spirit of the American freeman is already suspected to be timid, imitative, tame. Public and private avarice make the air we breathe thick and fat. The scholar is decent, indolent, complaisant. See already the tragic consequence. The mind of this country, taught to aim at low objects, eats upon itself. There is no work for any but the decorous and the complaisant. Young men of the fairest promise, who begin life upon our shores, inflated by the mountain winds, shined upon by all the stars of God, find the earth below not in unison with these, but are hindered from action by the disgust which the principles on which business is managed inspire, and turn drudges, or die of disgust, some of them suicides. What is the remedy? They did not yet see, and thousands of young men as hopeful now crowding to the barriers for the career do not yet see, that if the single man plant himself indomitably on his instincts, and there abide, the huge world will come round to him. Patience,—patience; with the shades of all the good and great for company; and for solace the perspective of your own infinite life; and for work the study and the communication of principles, the making those instincts prevalent, the conversion of the world. Is it not the chief disgrace in the world, not to be an unit;—not to be reckoned one character;—not to yield that peculiar fruit which each man was created to bear, but to be reckoned in the gross, in the hundred, or the thousand, of the party, the section, to which we belong; and our opinion predicted geographically, as the north, or the south? Not so, brothers and friends,—please God, ours shall not be so. We will walk on our own feet; we will work with our own hands; we will speak our own minds. The study of letters shall be no longer a name for piety, for doubt, and for sensual indulgence. The dread of man and the love of man shall be a wall of defence and a wreath of joy around all. A nation of men will for the first time exist, because each believes himself inspired by the Divine Soul which also inspires all men.

A year later he startled another Harvard audience by his Divinity Address, in which he broke with orthodox Unitarianism as he had formerly rebelled against Calvinism and Congregationalism. He analyzed the defects of historical

Christianity. He struck at the making of the Bible and Jesus fetishes—substitutes for original faith. God is always revealing himself: "It is the office of a true teacher to show that God is, not was; that He speaketh, not spake." Nothing can take the place of first-hand revelation: "Dare to love God without mediator or veil." As always he closed with a note of optimism and faith:

I look for the hour when that supreme Beauty, which ravished the souls of those eastern men, and chiefly of those Hebrews, and through their lips spoke oracles to all time, shall speak in the West also. The Hebrew and Greek Scriptures contain immortal sentences, that have been bread of life to millions. But they have no epical integrity; are fragmentary; are not shown in their order to the intellect. I look for the new Teacher, that shall follow so far those shining laws that he shall see them come full circle; shall see their rounding complete grace; shall see the world to be the mirror of the soul; shall see the identity of the law of gravitation with purity of heart; and shall show that the Ought, that Duty, is one thing with Science, with Beauty, and with Joy.

When these two addresses were published in a volume of essays that included "Self-Reliance," the reading public knew that a new and original force had appeared. As far away as Oxford, Matthew Arnold heard his voice along with those of Newman, Carlyle, and Goethe, and henceforth Concord was invested with a meaning like Weimar and Oxford. Society, he contended in "Self-Reliance," is "in conspiracy against the manhood of every one of its members." "Be a nonconformist." "Consistency is the hobgoblin of little minds." "Trust thyself: every heart vibrates to that iron string." "Never imitate." "Nothing is at last sacred but the integrity of your own mind." American youth responded to these ideas, all the more because the general public had so long fed on the worldly maxims of Franklin.

President Eliot said that every new idea he had tried to incorporate in his scheme of education—such as the elective system, or a chair of English literature—had been anticipated by the shrewd mystic of Concord. Dean Stanley said that he heard only one preacher in America, and that was Emerson, whose sayings were so universally quoted. Emerson just as definitely prophesied for America original genius in the fields of architecture, literature, and painting. He protested against the dominance of materialism in an oft-quoted passage: "Things are in the saddle and ride mankind."

VIII

Walt Whitman was Emerson raised to the *n*th degree. He tells of a conversation he had with Emerson on Boston Common when each had urged his point of view with much vigor, the older man trying to persuade the younger that in *Leaves of Grass* he had gone too far in discarding the reticence and restraint that poets had traditionally respected in the treatment of sex. Whitman replied that it was Emerson who had awakened him to the necessity of following one's instincts, and that he could do no other. Failing to agree, they went and had "a good dinner at the American House." Emerson would not have dared to invite him to a meeting of the Saturday Club at the same hotel, for Lowell, the arch critic, had already damned Whitman, and Whittier had thrown *Leaves of Grass* into the fire. Whitman would have felt even more ill at ease than Mark Twain did at a later time when he confronted the Brahmin writers at a celebrated dinner given in honor of Whittier. Emerson was, after all, in the New England tradition; he retained his connection with Harvard, was a good citizen of Concord and on friendly terms with his neighbors, and kept his balance between conservatism and radicalism. He was a sort of composite of Plato and Franklin. He was a prophet from within the established order, and the general effect was in the direction of reform rather than revolution—he was an Isaiah rather than an Amos.

Whitman, on the other hand, was an unmitigated individualist; he belonged neither to a college nor to a church, nor to any academy of letters, and he had no ties of family or party. If we now pay less attention than formerly to his frank treatment of sex, partly because the tide of public opinion has gone his way, it is because we realize that he visualized better than any other of our poets the physical background and the soul of America, that in his poems and in *Democratic Vistas* he gave new interpretations of democracy and freedom in fresh and unconventional forms of expression. He absorbed and assimilated the masses that he encountered on the ferries and busses of Manhattan, on his travels in all parts of the country, on the battlefields of Virginia, and in the hospitals of Washington. He looked down all roads, he shared the joys and sufferings of all classes, and he was a realization of his own dream of a *literatus,* a prophet, who would do for America what the poets of other lands had done for theirs.

He hailed the triumphs of inventions and sciences as the basis of larger spiritual resources. The completion of the first transcontinental railroad, the laying of the Atlantic cable, and the opening of the Suez Canal caught his imagination as showing the unity of the world. He was all but our first internationalist, and his poems "Passage to India,"

"Years of the Modern," and "Thou Mother with Thy
Equal Brood" antedated by forty years the speeches of
Woodrow Wilson. Columbus' dream was at least realized,
and East and West were united, one supplying the material
achievements and the other the Bibles and spiritual symbols
of ancient religions.

> The earth to be spann'd, connected by network,
> The races, neighbors, to marry and be given in marriage,
> The oceans to be cross'd, the distant brought near,
> The lands to be welded together....
> You, not for trade or transportation only,
> But in God's name, and for thy sake, O soul.

His imagination caught fire again when the Prince of
Wales and the first representatives of Japan visited New
York the same year. Again he saw America at the center of
the world, with all the obligations resting upon her to be the
mediator between the East and the West:

Brain of the New World, what a task is thine,
To formulate the Modern—out of peerless grandeur of the
    modern,
Out of thyself, comprising science, to recast poems, churches,
    art,
(Recast, may-be discard them, end them—may-be their work is
    done, who knows?)
By vision, hand, conception, on the background of the mighty
    past, the dead,
To limn with absolute faith the mighty living present.

Longfellow's celebrated passage, "Thou, too, sail on, O
Ship of State!" sounds a bit tame by the side of:

Sail, sail thy best, ship of Democracy,
Of value is thy freight, 'tis not the Present only,
The Past is also stored in thee,
Thou holdest not the venture of thyself alone, not of the
  Western continent alone,
Earth's *résumé* entire floats on thy keel O ship, is steadied by
  thy spars,
With thee Time voyages in trust, the antecedent nations sink
  or swim with thee,
With all their ancient struggles, martyrs, heroes, epics, wars,
  thou bear'st the other continents,
Theirs, theirs as much as thine, the destination-port triumphant;
Steer then with good strong hand and wary eye O helmsman,
  thou carriest great companions,
Venerable priestly Asia sails this day with thee,
And royal feudal Europe sails with thee.

If any one poem contains all of Whitman, it is "Years of
the Modern." It is a striking prophecy of what we like to
think is happening today—Wendell Willkie's "One World"
in free verse:

Years of the modern! years of the unperform'd!
Your horizon rises, I see it parting away for more august
  dramas,
I see not America only, not only Liberty's nation but other
  nations preparing,
I see tremendous entrances and exits, new combinations, the
  solidarity of races,
I see that force advancing with irrestible power on the world's
  stage,
(Have the old forces, the old wars, played their parts? are the
  acts suitable to them closed?)

I see Freedom, completely arm'd and victorious and very
haughty, with Law on one side and Peace on the other;
A stupendous trio all issuing forth against the idea of caste;
What historic denouements are these we so rapidly approach?
I see men marching and countermarching by swift millions,
I see the frontiers and boundaries of the old aristocracies
broken,
I see the landmarks of European Kings removed,
I see this day the People beginning their landmarks, (all others
give way;)
Never were such sharp questions ask'd as this day,
Never was average man, his soul, more energetic, more like a
God,
Lo, how he urges and urges, leaving the masses no rest!
His daring foot is on land and sea everywhere, he colonizes the
Pacific, the archipelagoes,
With the steamship, the electric telegraph, the newspaper, the
wholesale engines of war,
With these and the world-spreading factories he interlinks all
geography, all lands;
What whispers are these O lands, running ahead of you passing
under the seas?

Are not these words prophetic of the progress of the
United Nations toward a permanent organization for peace?

Are all nations communing? is there going to be but one heart
to the globe?
Is humanity forming en-masse? for lo, tyrants tremble, crowns
grow dim,
The earth, restive, confronts a new era, perhaps a general
divine war,
No one knows what will happen next, such portents fill the days
and nights;

Years prophetical! the space ahead as I walk, as I vainly try
to pierce it, is full of phantoms,
Unborn deeds, things soon to be, project their shapes around
me,
This incredible rush and heat, this strange ecstatic fever of
dreams O years!
Your dreams O years, how they penetrate through me! (I know
not whether I sleep or wake;)
The perform'd America and Europe grow dim, retiring in
shadow behind me.

In those lines is the prophecy of peace and brotherhood.
As we have already seen, this was one of the visions of the
later Hebrew prophets. Many English and American writers
have denounced war and envisaged universal peace, but
scarcely with the large perspective of Whitman. Swift, Bernard Shaw, and Mark Twain directed all their wit and sarcasm and cynicism at the absurdity and monstrosity of war.
Tennyson a hundred years ago, amid the radiant visions of
"Locksley Hall," gave expression to a possible league of
nations, a "Federation of the world"; and Longfellow at
almost the same time in "The Arsenal at Springfield" expressed the idea that the enormous sums of money expended
on battleships and armor might be better spent on schools,
colleges, and churches. And Robert Burns had already written not only the battle hymn of modern democracy but his
prophecy of the time when peace should reign throughout
the world in the famous lines:

> For a' that, an' a' that,
> It's comin yet for a' that,
> That man to man the world o'er
> Shall brithers be for a' that.

CHAPTER IV

REVEALERS OF BEAUTY, WONDER, AND MYSTERY

WE HAVE, for the most part, been considering religion in its sterner aspects—the inevitableness of the moral law, the struggle between good and evil forces in man and in the cosmic universe, and the prophetic treatment of religion as applied to social and political problems. Without minimizing these points of view, we are now to see religion as it relates to and includes beauty, wonder, and mystery; we are concerned with the riches of the inner life. In recent years the tendency among religious leaders has been to emphasize the social implications of religion and to develop to the maximum the reforming spirit in the Church. What we are apt to overlook is the personal aspect of the religious life, what, in Whitehead's fine phrase, man does with his solitariness, what he thinks and feels when he is left alone with himself and with God. After all, the Mount of Transfiguration and the secret places to which Jesus retired for prayer and meditation are necessary elements in any total conception of the Master's personality and influence.

Once more, as in other chapters, we take our point of departure from the Bible. Parallels to the writings which we shall consider in this chapter may be found in the Genesis hymn of creation, in many of the Psalms setting forth the glory and majesty of God, in the lyrics of the Song of Solomon with their radiant and buoyant expressions of physical

110

beauty and love, in the parables with their emphasis on the common things of earth and life, in the Sermon on the Mount with its striking use of figurative language, in Paul's hymn of faith, hope, and love, and in the representation of Jerusalem as embodying both the beauty of holiness and the holiness of beauty.

The book of Job is certainly one of the great books of the Bible, and, as Carlyle said, of world literature. The great problems of evil and suffering have never been more dramatically set forth, and yet the climax of the book—the speech of the Almighty out of the whirlwind—does not answer a single question raised by Job in the dark night of his spiritual anguish. In the most eloquent and long-sustained passage in English prose we find set forth the beauty of the natural world, the strength and wonder of the animal world, the mystery of light, the wideness of sea and sky. In other words, Job is made to feel that, while he has sought to understand one of the great mysteries of life, he does not realize that all things are shot through with mystery. This is one of the most emphatic expressions of the idea that, whatever else religion is, whatever demands it makes upon us, the sense of wonder and mystery is the very basis of worship. Such a passage must be put alongside other expressions of the fundamentals of religion, such as: "What doth the Lord require of thee, but to do justly, and to love mercy?" and, "Thou shalt love thy neighbour as thyself." "Consider the lilies of the field" is a glance into the beauty of the world and into the soul of religion.

II

So much must be said by way of introduction to the revelation that has been made, especially by poets, of "the wonder and bloom of the world." They have had the power to see all the various aspects of the world in which we live. Even those who have had little feeling for religious values have expressed what has come to them through their vivid realization of what the five senses brought to them. Men have sometimes rebelled against the asceticism of religion which would regard the natural world and natural passions as obstacles to the contemplation of the divine.

Charles Lamb in his "New Year's Eve" voiced his rebellion against the other-worldliness of those who long for death and Heaven. Some would regard it as a bit of paganism, but in its earth-hunger and its delight in the home, in friends, in books, it appeals to one important side of our nature:

I am not content to pass away "like a weaver's shuttle." Those metaphors solace me not, nor sweeten the unpalatable draught of mortality. I care not to be carried with the tide, that smoothly bears human life to eternity; and reluct at the inevitable course of destiny. I am in love with this green earth; the face of town and country; the unspeakable rural solitudes, and the sweet security of streets. I would set up my tabernacle here. I am content to stand still at the age to which I am arrived—I, and my friends: to be no younger, no richer, no handsomer. I do not want to be weaned by age; or drop, like mellow fruit, as they say, into the grave. Any alteration, on this earth of mine, in diet or in lodging, puzzles and discomposes me. My household gods plant a terrible fixed foot, and are not rooted up without blood. They do not willingly seek Lavinian shores. A new state of being staggers me.

Sun, and sky, and breeze, and solitary walks, and summer holidays, and the greenness of fields, and the delicious juices of meats and fishes, and society, and the cheerful glass, and candlelight, and fireside conversations, and innocent vanities and jests, and *irony itself*—do these things go out with life?

Can a ghost laugh, or shake his gaunt sides, when you are pleasant with him?

And you, my midnight darlings, my folios! must I part with the intense delight of having you (huge armfuls) in my embraces? Must knowledge come to me, if it come at all, by some awkward experiment of intuition, and no longer by this familiar process of reading?

Shall I enjoy friendships there, wanting the smiling indications which point me to them here, the recognisable face; "the sweet assurance of a look?"

Browning, as we shall see in the next chapter, was the most spiritual, the most Christian of poets, but his Fra Lippo Lippi rebels against medieval asceticism in words that express the heart's own feeling about nature, life, and art:

> If you get simple beauty and naught else,
> You get about the best thing God invents.

> However, you're my man, you've seen the world
> —The beauty and the wonder and the power,
> The shapes of things, their colors, lights and shades,
> Changes, surprises,—and God made it all!
> —For what? Do you feel thankful, ay or no,
> For this fair town's face, yonder river's line,
> The mountain round it and the sky above,
> Much more the figures of man, woman, child,
> These are the frame to? What's it all about?
> To be passed over, despised? or dwelt upon,
> Wondered at? oh, this last of course!—you say.
> But why not do as well as say,—paint these
> Just as they are, careless what comes of it?

113

God's works—paint any one, and count it crime
To let a truth slip.

. . . .

This world's no blot for us,
Nor blank; it means intensely, and means good:
To find its meaning is my meat and drink.

Even the greatest of medieval saints, Francis of Assisi,
wrote his "Canticle to the Sun" and looked upon the animals
and flowers as his brothers. The most Puritan of Puritans
wrote of the Palace Beautiful, the Arbor of Rest, the leaves
of the Tree of Life, and the Land of Beulah as necessary
stages in the progress of his pilgrims. Milton in his early
poems phrased the beauty of the English countryside at Horton, introduced into his pastoral elegy the most beautiful
flower passage in English poetry, and when he became blind
treasured in his imagination the fair places that he had seen
in Italy—the leaves falling upon the brooks of Vallombrosa
and the moon as he saw it through the telescope of Galileo.
Ruskin, who, as has been seen, became such a fierce prophet,
wrote about nature in every conceivable aspect; an anthology
of his descriptive passages is the most eloquent testimony to
the variety, richness, splendor, and majesty of the universe.
At the same time he wrote about architecture, painting, and
sculpture as still further revelations of beauty of form and
color. Even Carlyle sprinkled his *Sartor Resartus* and his other
prose writings with passages that surprise one accustomed
to his prophetic denunciations and lamentations. Nature was
one of the sources from which he gathered his insight into
symbols and hidden meanings. His "heroes" in *Heroes and
Hero Worship* were prophets, priests, men of action; but

the chapter on "The Hero as Poet" expresses well the difference between the poet and the prophet and the importance of Dante and Shakespeare in any pattern of spiritual life:

Poet and Prophet differ greatly in our loose modern notions of them. In some old languages, again, the titles are synonymous; *Vates* means both Prophet and Poet: and indeed at all times, Prophet and Poet, well understood, have much kindred of meaning. Fundamentally indeed they are still the same; in this most important respect especially. That they have penetrated both of them into the sacred mystery of the Universe; what Goethe calls "the open secret." "Which is the great secret?" asks one.—"The *open* secret,"—open to all, seen by almost none! That divine mystery, which lies everywhere in all Beings, "the Divine Idea of the World, that which lies at the bottom of Appearance," as Fichte styles it; of which all Appearance, from the starry sky to the grass of the field, but especially the Appearance of man and his work, is but the *vesture,* the embodiment that renders it visible. This divine mystery *is* in all times and in all places; veritably is. In most times and places it is greatly overlooked; and the Universe, definable always in one or the other dialect, as the realised Thought of God, is considered a trivial, inert, commonplace matter,—as if, says the Satirist, it were a dead thing, which some upholsterer had put together! It could do no good at present, to *speak* much about this; but it is a pity for every one of us if we do not know it, live ever in the knowledge of it. Really a most mournful pity; a failure to live at all, if we live otherwise!

But now, I say, whoever may forget this divine mystery, the *Vates,* whether Prophet or Poet has penetrated into it; is a man sent hither to make it more impressively known to us. That always is his message; he is to reveal that to us,—that sacred mystery which he more than others lives ever present with. While others forget it, he knows it;— I might say, he has been driven to know it; without consent asked of *him,* he finds himself living in it, bound to live in it. Once more, here is no Hearsay, but a direct Insight and Belief; this man too could not help being a sincere man! Whosoever may live in the shows of things, it is for him a necessity of nature to live in the very fact of things. A man once more, in earnest with the Universe, though all others were but toying with it. He is a *Vates,* first of all, in virtue of being sincere. So far Poet and Prophet, participators in the "open secret," are one.

With respect to their distinction again: The *Vates* Prophet, we might say, has seized that sacred mystery rather on the moral side, as Good and Evil, Duty and Prohibition; the *Vates* Poet on what the Germans call the aesthetic side, as beautiful, and the like. The one we call a revealer of what we are to do, the other of what we are to love. But indeed these two provinces run into one another, and cannot be disjoined. The Prophet too has his eye on what we are to love: how else shall he know what it is we are to do? The highest Voice ever heard on this earth said withal, "Consider the lilies of the field; they toil not, neither do they spin: yet Solomon in all his glory was not arrayed like one of these." A glance, that, into the deepest deep of Beauty. "The lilies of the field,"—dressed finer than earthly princes, springing-up there in the humble furrow-field; a beautiful *eye* looking-out on you, from the great inner Sea of Beauty! How could the rude Earth make these, if her Essence, rugged as she looks and is, were not inwardly Beauty? In this point of view, too, a saying of Goethe's, which has staggered several, may have meaning: "The Beautiful," he intimates, "is higher than the Good; the Beautiful includes in it the Good."

Emerson, with all his emphasis on self-reliance and his exhortations for the courage of individuality, began his career with an essay on "Nature," which is perhaps our

most complete expression of what nature means to man
from the most practical use to the most ethereal contemplation of truth. It was certainly the basis of his transcendental
interpretation of nature; it was a veritable symbol of the
"Over-Soul," which is but another name for the Holy
Spirit.

Beauty is the mark God sets upon virtue. . . .
The world thus exists to the soul to satisfy the desire of
beauty. This element I call an ultimate end. No reason can be
asked or given why the soul seeks beauty. Beauty, in its largest
and profoundest sense, is one expression for the universe. God
is the all-fair. Truth, and goodness, and beauty are but different
faces of the same All. But beauty in nature is not ultimate. It is
the herald of inward and eternal beauty, and is not alone a
solid and satisfactory good. It must stand as a part, and not as
yet the last or highest expression of the final cause of Nature.

III

We can understand better the interpretation of beauty if
we see it in a somewhat isolated form rather than in any
philosophical interpretation such as that of Carlyle or Emerson. It is generally agreed that John Keats was pre-eminently
the poet of beauty. In a revolutionary age, in which writers
were profundly concerned with the social and political problems raised by the French and American revolutions, he
built a temple of beauty. With the materials furnished by
Greek myth, legend, and poetry, with his absorption of
medieval legends and art, with his increasing appreciation
of Shakespeare and his contemporaries, and, above all, with
his sensitiveness to nature, he illustrates, without any suggestion of the didactic, his three most frequently quoted
passages, "The poetry of earth is never dead," "A thing of

117

beauty is a joy for ever," and, "Beauty is truth, truth beauty." In the opening lines of *Endymion* he elaborates the sources and meaning of beauty as found in nature and in romantic stories:

> A thing of beauty is a joy for ever:
> Its loveliness increases; it will never
> Pass into nothingness: but still will keep
> A bower quiet for us, and a sleep
> Full of sweet dreams, and health, and quiet breathing.
> Therefore, on every morrow, are we wreathing
> A flowery band to bind us to the earth,
> Spite of despondence, of the inhuman dearth
> Of noble natures, of the gloomy days,
> Of all the unhealthy and o'er-darkened ways
> Made for our searching: yes, in spite of all,
> Some shape of beauty moves away the pall
> From our dark spirits. Such the sun, the moon,
> Trees old, and young, sprouting a shady boon
> For simple sheep; and such are daffodils
> With the green world they live in; and clear rills
> That for themselves a cooling covert make
> 'Gainst the hot season; the mid forest brake,
> Rich with a sprinkling of fair musk-rose blooms:
> And such too is the grandeur of the dooms
> We have imagined for the mighty dead;
> All lovely tales that we have heard or read:
> An endless fountain of immortal drink,
> Pouring unto us from the heaven's brink.

Now the basis of his sense and appreciation of beauty was a rare awareness, alertness, of his five senses. No poet has surpassed him in his expressions of color, melody, taste, and odor. He explored the world of sensations. There is no

such color passage in English poetry as his description of
Madeline's room in "The Eve of St. Agnes," and especially
of the high and triple-arched casement,

> All garlanded with carven imag'ries . . .
> And diamonded with panes of quaint device,
> Innumerable of stains and splendid dyes, . . .
> And twilight saints, and dim emblazonings.

Matching this splendor of color were the "warm gules on
Madeline's fair breast," with "rose-bloom" on her hands and
"soft amethyst" on her silver cross, and "on her hair a
glory, like a saint." In the same poem there is the exquisite
feast prepared for Madeline by her lover, with a sort of
magical food brought from faraway places:

> And lucent syrops, tinct with cinnamon;
> Manna and dates, in argosy transferr'd
> From Fez, and spiced dainties, every one,
> From silken Samarcand to cedar'd Lebanon.

It is like the passage on wine in the "Ode to a Nightingale"
—wine "cool'd a long age in the deep-delved earth," with
suggestions of the fountain of the gods and the harvests of
southern France. In the same poem there is the ecstasy arising
from the song of the bird as it sings of summer "in full-
throated ease." It becomes in his imagination the bird that
has sung through the centuries—

> Perhaps the self-same song that found a path
> Through the sad heart of Ruth,

and that in the *Arabian Nights*

> Charm'd magic casements, opening on the foam
> Of perilous seas, in faery lands forlorn.

His vivid realization of the scenes represented on the vase in the "Ode on a Grecian Urn"—the lovers at the point of ecstatic rapture, the shepherd piping his spiritual ditties, the procession of the worshipers to a sacrifice in the temple— his apostrophe "To Autumn" as the "season of mists and mellow fruitfulness," . . .

> While barred clouds bloom the soft-dying day,
> And touch the stubble-plains

—all these and many more testify to an almost pagan sense of joy and beauty. When someone asked Shelley why Keats wrote so many poems and passages about Greek legends and myths, he replied, "He is a Greek." That was why in his "Sleep and Poetry" Keats condemns in an exaggerated way the pseudo-classic period of English literature as blind and deaf to the beauty of nature.

> The winds of heaven blew, the ocean roll'd
> Its gathering waves—ye felt it not. The blue
> Bar'd its eternal bosom, and the dew
> Of summer nights collected still to make
> The morning precious: beauty was awake!
> Why were ye not awake? But ye were dead
> To things ye knew not of.

This denunciation, which is paralleled by Wordsworth's sonnet "The world is too much with us," might well be applied to many Christians who have not appreciated the beauty and wonder of the world in which they live. On the other hand, this exquisite sensuousness that we find in Keats has often led to an extreme form of aestheticism, to sheer pagan delight. Epicureanism has often resulted from this tendency to isolate sheer beauty. *A Shropshire Lad,* especially in the poem on the cherry tree; many of the poems of Edna St. Vincent Millay, especially "Renascence" and "Autumn"; William Morris' "The Idle Singer of an Empty Day"; Walter Pater's famous conclusion to his *Studies in the History of the Renaissance*—all represent a feeling for beauty but without any significance of its deeper symbolism.

IV

Nearly all of the contemporaries of Keats share the "renascence of wonder" that was characteristic of the Romantic period of English literature (1798-1832). With all of Byron's cynicism and pessimism, with all his mockery of sacred themes, he had the power to be moved by great things in nature, in art, in history. Lacking Keats's sensitiveness to the more delicate aspects of nature, he felt as few men have the glory of the mountains and the sea, both of which inspired some of his most eloquent passages in *Childe Harold*. During the summer of 1816 he fell under the spell of Lake Leman (Geneva) and the Alps, writing especially of a moonlight night on the lake and of a storm in the Alps. He once wrote that the mountains and the ocean were his altars; he certainly felt the presence of the eternal, the infinite:

> Not vainly did the early Persian make
> His altar the high places and the peak
> Of earth-o'ergazing mountains, and thus take
> A fit and unwalled temple, there to seek
> The Spirit in whose honor shrines are weak,
> Upreared of human hands. Come, and compare
> Columns and idol-dwellings, Goth or Greek,
> With Nature's realms of worship, earth and air,
> Nor fix on fond abodes to circumscribe thy prayer!

121

Again he writes of the transcendent mood that came over him:

> All heaven and earth are still—though not in sleep,
> But breathless, as we grow when feeling most;
> And silent, as we stand in thoughts too deep:—
> All heaven and earth are still: From the high host
> Of stars, to the lull'd lake and mountain-coast,
> All is concenter'd in a life intense,
> Where not a beam, nor air, nor leaf is lost,
> But hath a part of being, and a sense
> Of that which is of all Creator and defense.
>
> Then stirs the feeling infinite, so felt
> In solitude, where we are *least* alone;
> A truth, which through our being then doth melt
> And purifies from self; it is a tone,
> The soul and source of music, which makes known
> Eternal harmony, and sheds a charm,
> Like to the fabled Cytherea's zone,
> Binding all things with beauty;—'twould disarm
> The spectre Death, had he substantial power to harm.

In the midst of some of his most cynical and even blasphemous passages in *Don Juan* he writes the beautiful prayer beginning "Ave Maria! blessed be the hour!" It is the twilight, the vesper hour when he feels the presence of the Madonna and her Son; even "the forest leaves seem'd stirr'd with prayer" while "the deep bell in the distant tower" sounds the Angelus. The vesper bells awaken memories and suggest the brooding wings of the parent bird; he thinks of those who sail the seas or wend as pilgrims on the way of life. He is aware of

> all that springs from the great Whole,
> Who hath produced, and will receive the soul.

In the oft-quoted and hackneyed apostrophe to the ocean at the end of *Childe Harold,* he sees not only the wreck of the seven empires around the Mediterranean—the best illustration of the note that runs throughout the poem of the repetition of the cycles of history—but he sees in the ocean

> The image of Eternity—the throne
> Of the Invisible.

Such as creation's dawn beheld, thou rollest now.

V

With far less dross in his make-up than Byron and with far more of the ethereal, Shelley was particularly sensitive throughout his life to the infinite significance of nature as a revelation of something behind and in the universe. Nourished by clear dream and solemn vision, and influenced by Plato's doctrine of ideas, he expressed in many poems the idea embodied in his "Hymn to Intellectual Beauty":

> The awful shadow of some unseen Power
>   Floats tho' unseen amongst us,—visiting
>   This various world with as inconstant wing
> As summer winds that creep from flower to flower,
>
>   .   .   .   .
>
> Like hues and harmonies of evening,—
>   Like clouds in starlight widely spread,—
>   Like memory of music fled,—
>   Like aught that for its grace may be
> Dear, and yet dearer for its mystery.

123

This spirit of beauty is identical with that of love, and they are two manifestations of what Emerson calls the "Over-Soul." The climax of "Adonais" is an expression of the idea that "the One remains, the many change and pass," and that earth's shadows are but a suggestion of heaven's light. Borne along by his memory of Keats and his visualization of the beauty and wonder of nature and of the great poets who have lived before, he reaches a state of ecstasy in which the infinite is seen in its various manifestations:

> That Light whose smile kindles the Universe,
> That Beauty in which all things work and move,
> That Benediction which the eclipsing Curse
> Of birth can quench not, that sustaining Love
> Which thro' the web of being blindly wove
> By man and beast and earth and air and sea
> Burns bright or dim, as each are mirrors of
> The fire for which all thirst: now beams on me
> Consuming the last clouds of cold mortality.

In a passage that anticipates his death a year later, he reaches a stage of transfiguration in which he passes from earth in his spirit's bark which takes him

> Far from the shore, far from the trembling throng
> Whose sails were never to the tempest given,

and thus reaches a state of exaltation which comes to mortals only in the supreme moments of vision. Few men have been more conscious of what Christians call the Holy Spirit.

VI

Of all the poets of the Romantic period Wordsworth was pre-eminently the poet of nature. He added a whole region of England to the imagination and heart of English-speaking people. He was more realistic than Shelley, more truly devout than Byron, more spiritual than Keats. Coleridge expressed better than anyone else his distinctive purpose and function:

Mr. Wordsworth . . . was to propose to himself as his object, to give the charm of novelty to things of every day, and to excite a feeling analogous to the supernatural, by awakening the mind's attention from the lethargy of custom, and directing it to the loveliness and the wonders of the world before us; an inexhaustible treasure, but for which, in consequence of the film of familiarity and selfish solicitude, we have eyes, yet see not, ears that hear not, and hearts that neither feel nor understand.

Wordsworth had a vision of nature as the revelation of God and as the teacher and comforter of man. In his "Intimations of Immortality" man comes from his home in the skies "trailing clouds of glory." He has the heritage of an eternal life. To the infant's eye the world is

> Apparelled in celestial light,
> The glory and the freshness of a dream.

Wordsworth himself, as we see in the account of his boyhood in *The Prelude,* was a child developing under the influence of nature, which kept his soul allied with the divine life; in the stealing of bird's nests, in skating, in rowing, and other normal sports of England he felt the invisible presence of nature's loveliness. At first there was a physical pleasure in nature, a sensuous joy; then it spoke to him of "unremembered pleasure"; then he heard in it "the still, sad music of humanity"; and finally he came to feel in nature

a sense sublime
Of something far more deeply interfused,
Whose dwelling is the light of setting suns,
And the round ocean and the living air,
And the blue sky, and in the mind of man;
A motion and a spirit, that impels
All thinking things, all object of all thought,
And rolls through all things.

This passage in "Tintern Abbey" is the supreme expression in literature of the universal divine presence; here the poet caught a vision of that life that is in the meanest flower that blows. In his shorter poems the butterfly was the "historian of my infancy"; the discovery of the celandine was fraught with as much pleasure as the astronomer feels in the discovery of a new star; the daisy was an apostle of truth as he met it in the retired places of earth; the daffodils caused his heart to dance with joy; a sunrise was the moment of dedication to new ideals of life; the evening sunset seemed the stairway on which his soul could mount into the heavens. When the fierce storm of the French Revolution had passed over him, wrecking his hopes and producing chaos in his soul, he turned to nature for consolation. He was nature's high priest, and all who read him will find themselves looking with new interest upon the manifold beauties of the universe. To an age of materialism he was a revealer of spiritual life; to an age of doubt and skepticism he brought the calm and rest of a sublime faith in God and man and nature.

But it is not simply nature that we discover in Wordsworth. He was the poet of the "god-like hours" of the soul. Nature was simply one of the sources of such high communion. He reached such a state of spiritual ecstasy many

times in his life, and especially in three poems written almost ten years apart, "Tintern Abbey," "Intimations of Immortality," and "An Evening of Extraordinary Splendour
and Beauty." The mood in which he reached the heights of
mystical vision was expressed in the first poem in these
words:

> That blessed mood,
> In which the burthen of the mystery,
> In which the heavy and the weary weight
> Of all this unintelligible world,
> Is lightened:—that serene and blessed mood,
> In which the affections gently lead us on,-
> Until, the breath of this corporeal frame
> And even the motion of our human blood
> Almost suspended, *we are laid asleep*
> *In body, and become a living soul:*
> While with an eye made quiet by the power
> Of harmony, and the deep power of joy,
> We see into the life of things.

This power is lost sight of in the ordinary course of life,
but there are moments when the vision of the infinite is restored, when the obstinate questionings of sense and outward things, the high instincts, the truths that wake to perish
never, reassert themselves, and we become aware of the
possible reaches of the human spirit. Such transcendent
moods correspond to the high moments of nature, especially
when we have the blending of sunset and mountain and the
mood of solitude and prayer. Wordsworth closed his poetic
career by describing such an experience:

> From worlds not quickened by the sun
> A portion of the gift is won;

127

> An intermingling of Heaven's pomp is spread
> On ground which British shepherds tread.

He realized the meaning of Jacob's ladder whereon angels ascended and descended. The sensation of childlike wonder was renewed, as if "by miracle restored." His soul rejoiced in a second birth, even though the "visionary splendour" soon passed away.

VII

Of nature as a revelation of the divine and of the transcendent moods to which such contemplation leads, Sidney Lanier's "Sunrise" and "The Marshes of Glynn" are striking examples. In a way they may be considered as the furthest reach of nineteenth-century romanticism or idealism. The marshes of these poems are about the ugliest things in nature, except when the tide is at its height and they blend with the sea. Lanier prepares for the great experience described in the second poem by spending a hot summer day in the forest of live-oaks that borders the marshes. In the glooms of the trees he has found "closets of lone desire," "wildwood privacies" that have been as cells for prayer; the sunbeam shining through the thick foliage has seemed "like a lane into heaven." When he steps from the forest, he faces "the vast sweet visage of space"; his soul, "grown to a lordly great compass," responds to the sky, the sea, the beach, the marsh hen, and above all the sunset. The greatness of God is like "the range of the marshes, the liberal marshes of Glynn." The climax of the poem comes when the full tide is in and "the sea and the marsh are one":

> And the sea lends large, as the marsh: lo, out of his plenty the sea
> Pours fast: full soon the time of flood-tide must be:

Look how the grace of the sea doth go
About and about through the intricate channels that flow
    Here and there,
        Everywhere,
Till his waters have flooded the uttermost creeks and the low-
    lying lanes,
And the marsh is meshed with a million veins,
That like as with rosy and silvery essences flow
  In the rose-and-silver evening glow.
        Farewell, my lord Sun!
The creeks overflow: a thousand rivulets run
'Twixt the roots of the sod; the blades of the marsh-grass stir;
Passeth a hurrying sound of wings that westward whirr;
Passeth, and all is still; and the currents cease to run;
And the sea and the marsh are one.
How still the plains of the waters be!
The tide is in his ecstasy.
The tide is at his highest height:
        And it is night.

Then comes the comparison of the tide to the subconscious,
or rather the interpenetration of the divine and the human:

And now from the Vast of the Lord will the waters of sleep
Roll in on the souls of men,
But who will reveal to our waking ken
The forms that swim and the shapes that creep
        Under the waters of sleep?
And I would I could know what swimmeth below when the
    tide comes in
On the length and the breadth of the marvellous marshes of
    Glynn.

What Lanier found in nature, he also found in music:
"music is Love in search of a word" was his way of saying

that music is of all the arts that which comes nearest to expressing the inexpressible. His "Symphony" is music's condemnation of the spirit of trade. Browning in "Abt Vogler" has best expressed the mood of rapture and insight which a great musician can reach. Abt Vogler is playing an organ after his pupils have left him alone. Suddenly he realizes that he is in the full glow of creative power—he does something he has never done before. He sees arising before his vision a magical palace or temple, broad-based and reaching toward the sky. Novel splendors burst forth: "For earth had attained to Heaven, there was no more near nor far." All this through his mastery of the keys of the organ. It is so wonderful that the dead come back to life, even as Elias and Moses came to the Mount of Transfiguration. Here is a flash of the will that can. Musicians are nearer the Creator than poets or artists; they transcend technique, for they can make out of three sounds "not a fourth sound, but a star." Such an hour must pass, but he consoles himself with the fact that such experiences can be treasured in the soul and are a foregleam of immortality:

All we have willed or hoped or dreamed of good shall exist;
  Not its semblance, but itself; no beauty, nor good, nor power
Whose voice has gone forth, but each survives for the melodist
  When eternity affirms the conception of an hour.
The high that proved too high, the heroic for earth too hard,
  The passion that left the ground to lose itself in the sky,
Are music sent up to God by the lover and the bard;
  Enough that he heard it once: we shall hear it by and by.

It is very characteristic of Browning that the musician feels his way back to the earth again—"the C Major of this life." He was a mystic with his feet on the ground.

VIII

Edward Dowden had this poem in mind when he compared Tennyson, Wordsworth, and Browning with respect to their mysticism:

Accordingly, although we find the idea of God entering largely into the poetry of Mr. Tennyson, there is little recognition of special contact of the soul with the divine Being in any supernatural way of quiet or of ecstasy. This precludes all spiritual rapture, that glorious folly, that heavenly madness, wherein true wisdom is acquired. Wordsworth in some of his solitary trances of thought really entered into the frame of mind which the mystic knows as union or as ecstasy, when thought expires into enjoyment. With Mr. Tennyson the mystic is always the visionary who suffers from an overexcitable fancy. The nobler aspects of the mystical religious spirit are unrepresented in his poetry.

Undoubtedly Mr. Dowden is right in the main in his contention that the nobler of the mystical religious spirit are more noticeable in Wordsworth or Browning than in Tennyson; but to say that they are not represented in his poetry is very far from the truth. We shall see, as we go along, that there are many passages in which the higher moods of the soul are expressed; and from the full and accurate *Memoir* by his son we know that religious ecstasy was a very characteristic mood in Tennyson's life. In his letters and diary and in the reminiscences of his friends we have many prose commentaries on passages in his poetry. Hallam Tennyson says of the experience of his father:

Throughout his life he had a constant feeling of spiritual harmony existing between ourselves and the outward visible

131

universe, and of the actual immanence of God in the infinitesimal atom as in the vastest system. He would say, "The soul seems to me one with God; how, I cannot tell."

The poet himself wrote to a friend at one time:

A kind of waking trance I have frequently had, quite up from boyhood, when I have been all alone. This has generally come through repeating my own name two or three times to myself silently till all at once, as it were out of the intensity of the consciousness of individuality itself seemed to dissolve and fade away into boundless being; and this, not a confused state, but the clearest of the clearest, the surest of the surest, the weirdest of the weirdest, utterly beyond words, where death was almost a laughable impossibility—the loss of personality, if so it were, seeming no extinction, but the only true life.

This might, he said, be the state which Paul describes, "whether in the body, I cannot tell; or whether out of the body, I cannot tell." He was ashamed of such a feeble description, for his experience under such circumstances was altogether incommunicable.

In 1869, while writing "The Holy Grail," he also made to his family the following significant utterance:

Yes, it is true that there are moments when the flesh is nothing to me, when I feel and know the flesh to be the vision, God and the spiritual the only real and true. Depend upon it, the spiritual is the real; it belongs to one more than the hand and the foot. You may tell me that my hand and my foot are only imaginary symbols of my existence. I could believe you; but you never, never can convince me that the I is not an eternal reality, and that the spiritual is not the true and real part of me.

132

These words he spoke with such passionate earnestness that a solemn silence fell on the family as he left the room. In a letter to Emily Sellwood, who afterward became his wife, he also says:

To me, often, the far-off world seems nearer than the present, for in the present is always something unreal and indistinct; but the other seems a good solid planet, rolling around its great hills and paradises to the harmony of more steadfast laws. There steam up from about me mists of weakness, or sin, or despondency, and roll between me and the far planets, but it is there still.

As he grew older, Tennyson felt more and more the reality of the unseen. Edward FitzGerald gives this interesting observation:

I remember A. T. admiring the abstracted look of a Murillo Madonna at Dulwich, the eyes of which are on you, but seem "looking at something beyond, beyond the actual into abstraction." This has been noticed of some great men; it is the trance of the seer. I do not remember seeing it in A. T. himself, great as he was from top to toe, and his eyes dark, powerful, and severe.

But FitzGerald afterward changed his mind, and wrote: "I have seen it in his [A.T.'s]. Some American spoke of the same in Wordsworth." Yes, with Tennyson's deepening life came a greater realization of the transcendent moods of the human soul, a greater spiritual power that expressed itself in the eye and tone of voice, and in more elevated poetry. Speaking of him two years before his death, his son says:

While he talked of the mystery of the universe his face, full of the strong lines of thought, was lighted up, and his words glowed as it were with inspiration. In 1888 we are told that during the day he lay on his sofa, near the south window of his study, and told us that looking out on the great landscape he had wonderful thoughts about God and the universe, and felt as if looking into the other world.

All of these passages, and others that might be quoted, show that not always, perhaps, but in his greater moments Tennyson did know something of "That heavenly madness wherein true wisdom is acquired." He did not look upon the mystic as a "visionary who suffers from an overexcitable fancy." He was terribly in earnest about the significance of such moments in his life. He said, with something of the same vigor that he used in speaking of immortality: "By God Almighty there is no delusion in the matter. It is no nebulous ecstasy but a state of transcendent wonder associated with absolute clearness of mind."

And yet Tennyson was far from being a spiritualist. We have an account of a conversation between him and his brother Fredrick, in which he said:

I grant you that spiritualism must not be judged by its quacks; but I am convinced that God and the ghosts of men would choose something other than mere table legs through which to speak to the heart of man. You tell me that my duty is to give up everything, in order to propagate spiritualism. There is really too much flummery mixed up with it, supposing, as I am inclined to believe, there is something in it.

It may be seen from this that Tennyson had little sympathy with the extreme views of many modern mystics. His mysticism was based upon reality.

Perhaps the best short statement of Tennyson's faith in

the unseen is found in "The Higher Pantheism." He wrote it for the Metaphysical Society of London, and meant it, no doubt, as a protest against the materialism and agnosticism of many of the members of that interesting organization. It is full of the idealism of Plato and Goethe:

The sun, the moon, the stars, the seas, the hills and the plains—
Are not these, O Soul, the vision of Him who reigns?

With this God, of whom we catch but broken gleams, we can hold personal communion in prayer:

Speak to Him thou for He hears, and Spirit with Spirit can
    meet—
Closer is He than breathing, and nearer than hands and feet.

These lines might serve as the commentary on the ninety-fourth canto of *In Memoriam,* which is an account of the mingling of Tennyson's soul with the universal soul in a moment of transcendent ecstasy or rapture. The passage has been very much misunderstood. In the first edition it read:

And all at once it seem'd at last
    His living soul was flash'd on mine,

And mine in *his* was wound, and whirl'd
    About empyreal heights of thoughts.

Unquestionably the logic of the preceding cantos was in favor of this reading, but in a later edition Tennyson changed it so that it has a much wider application. It comes as the climax of a long line of thought and feeling. After he has considered the questions of immortality and fame and has longed, as few men have longed, for the spirit of Hallam, one summer night as he reads the letters of his dead friend he is lifted up into the spiritual world. All that has gone before has prepared him for the realization in a supreme degree of the spirit of God in his soul:

> And all at once it seem'd at last
> *The* living soul was flash'd on mine,

> And mine in *this* was wound, and whirl'd
> About empyreal heights of thought,
> And came on that which is, and caught
> The deep pulsations of the world,

> Æonian music measuring out
> The steps of Time.

.   .   .   .

> Vague words! but ah, how hard to frame
> In matter-moulded forms of speech,
> Or ev'n for intellect to reach
> Thro' memory that which I became.

In "The Two Voices" we have many suggestions of Wordsworth's "Intimations of Immortality." The argument for a pre-existence is tentatively advanced; at least the man uses it as an answer to the first voice, which says that "to begin implies an end." In certain great moments of life there are impressions that seem to carry us back, as in a trance, to that imperial palace whence we came before God shut the doorway of the head. One does feel, now and then, emotions that connect him with a world other than this— moments corresponding to the "calm weather" of Wordsworth's Ode":

> Some vague emotion of delight
> In gazing up an Alpine height,

Some yearning toward the lamps of night.

.　　.　　.　　.　　.　　.

Moreover, something is or seems,
That touches me with mystic gleams,
Like glimpses of forgotten dreams—

Of something felt, like something here;
Of something done, I know not where;
Such as no language may declare.

Another poem in which the rapture of the human soul is
well expressed is "The Ancient Sage." That the experience
described in it is not altogether dramatic is proved by the
words of Tyndall. One night Tyndall, Jowett, and Tennyson were talking together. Says Tyndall:

Tennyson described to me a state of consciousness into which
he could throw himself by thinking intensely of his own name.
It was an apparent isolation of the spirit from the body. Wish-
ing doubtless to impress upon me the reality of the phenomena,
he exclaimed that it was a state of transcendent wonder. This
trance, he claimed, was a union with God such as that described by Plotinus and Porphyry, and is the best argument
against materialism and in favor of personal immortality.

A few months after this conversation Tyndall saw that he
had given expression to the same idea in "The Ancient
Sage." In the poem an old sage, "a thousand summers ere
the time of Christ," is talking with a skeptical young
man who has in his hands a poem expressing the vanity of
life and the darkness of the world. Against the words of the
poem the ancient seer pleads for the "Nameless," notwithstanding the fact that his existence cannot be proved; he be-

lieves also in the final triumph of the good, and that the doors of night are the gates of light:

> And more, my son! for more than once when I
> Sat all alone, revolving in myself
> The word that is the symbol of myself,
> The mortal limit of the Self was loosed,
> And past into the Nameless, as a cloud
> Melts into heaven. I touch'd my limbs, the limbs
> Were strange, not mine—and yet no shade of doubt,
> But utter clearness, and thro' loss of Self
> The gain of such large life as match'd with ours
> Were Sun to star—unshadowable in words,
> Themselves but shadows of a shadow-world.

He closes his rapturous address to the young man, who can no longer reply to him, with words that are a suggestion of the Transfiguration:

> But curb the beast would cast thee in the mire,
> And leave the hot swamp of voluptuousness
> A cloud between the Nameless and thyself,
> And lay thine uphill shoulder to the wheel,
> And climb the Mount of Blessing, when, if thou
> Look higher, then—perchance—thou mayest—beyond
> A hundred ever-rising mountain lines,
> And past the range of Night and Shadow—see
> The high-heaven dawn of more than mortal day
> Strike on the Mount of Vision

Is this vague mysticism? we ask; and we answer again, with great emphasis, No. It is the genuine mysticism of Wordsworth and Browning. Tennyson has given us in his poetry many expressions of a false mysticism. He understood, as few men have, the evil that may come from false

138

ideas of religion, and has entered his protest in memorable words against a hollow idealism.

The poem "St. Simeon Stylites" must occur to anyone in thinking on this subject. If one has always thought of Tennyson as a dilettante poet—faultily faultless, icily regular—he surely has not read this vigorous and wholesome poem. We see St. Simeon on his pillar of stone, "from scalp to sole one slough and crust of sin," and hear him "battering the gates of heaven with storms of prayer," as he yearns for the white robes and the palms that will atone for all of this self-mortification and torture. Even now, at times, he sees an angel standing watching; his one great object is to subdue his flesh that he may be more alone with God:

> Is that the angel there
> That holds a crown? Come, blessed brother, come.
> I know thy glittering face. I waited long.

This is his beatific vision—a vision of God that comes from denying this world and living on in the other—and we say with the poet that it is a hollow mockery.

The noble phases of the medieval religion are presented in "St. Agnes' Eve" and "Sir Galahad." Beautiful and romantic as these poems are, however, they suggest by way of contrast the healthier and saner religion of the poet and seer of the nineteenth century. From the casement of the monastery, in the first poem, the nun, looking out on the beautiful snow that envelops the earth, and at the stars that shed a mild, beneficent light over all the winter scene, has a vision of the Bridegroom. In "Sir Galahad" the vision of the Holy Grail, afterward so finely developed in one of the idyls, is suggested. All his heart is drawn above. Mightier transports than love move and thrill him. When at last he catches the vision of the Holy Grail, he exclaims:

Ah, blessed vision! blood of God!
My spirit beats her mortal bars.

IX

We are unavoidably reminded of the legend of the Holy Grail as interpreted by Tennyson. It is the idyl that is oftenest neglected and misunderstood, and yet it is in many senses the most significant of all. Although it may lack the moving pathos of "Guinevere" or the solemn majesty of "Morte d'Arthur" and the beautiful narrative style of "Lancelot and Elaine," it is the idyl in which Tennyson has treated the religious problem of his age with greatest power. He himself regarded it as his highest utterance on life. It was the hardest one for him to write; but when it did come to him, it came like the inspiration of a prophet. I doubt not that his difficulty in writing it was due to the greatness of the theme which he presents.

There are visions and visions in this idyl—trances, ecstasies, raptures. It is therefore an especially good illustration of the study we have been making. Not Francis of Assisi nor Augustine ever had more glorious visions of the blessed life or the city of God than Galahad and Percivale and the holy nun. Other parts of the Idyls do not so thoroughly reproduce the medieval atmosphere out of which these legends came; but the religious fervor of the Middle Ages, that long-told story of the Holy Grail, is well portrayed in this poem. It is not necessary to rehearse the story of the Holy Grail; I shall use only so much of it as is needed for the understanding of the point at issue. The maid sister of

Percivale, disappointed in love, has turned her attention only
to holy things. While passion is raging in Arthur's court—
the terrible passion of unholy love—she holds herself aloof
from it all, and gives herself to fasting and alms. Her teacher
has inspired her with zeal for a vision of the Holy Grail, and
at last she catches a glimpse of it. Her eyes, beautiful in the
light of holiness, shine with a glory never before known;
she tells her brother of the sound as of a silver horn from
over the hills. No music of earth was ever like it:

> And down the long beam stole the Holy Grail,
> Rose-red with beatings in it, as if alive,
> Till all the white walls of my cell were dyed
> With rosy colors leaping on the wall.

Galahad's eyes become like her own, when he hears of the
vision—Galahad, the beautiful youth begotten by enchant-
ment. He is sent forth by the maiden:

> Go forth, for thou shalt see what I have seen,
> And break thro' all, till one will crown thee king
> Far in the spiritual city.

When on a summer night the Holy Grail, clad in a luminous cloud, appears to them all in the banquet hall, all the
knights swear to follow it. In the tournament on the next
day Galahad and Percivale are successful because strength
is with them from the vision. The story is a long one of the
disappointments of the various knights—their fruitless search
for the vision which appears to them in so many different
ways and at last brings gloom to their lives. The height of
medieval ecstasy is in Sir Galahad's vision as he passes away
into the spiritual city, the veritable city of God that Augus-

tine saw with his enraptured eye or that John beheld from Patmos. The vision has never failed from his sight, moving with him night and day. Through the night it has been a veritable pillar of fire, and at last in a vision of glory it leads him to the throne of God. From the swamp and dark places of earth Percivale sees him passing to the spiritual city, with all her spires and gateways in a glory like one pearl.

> And from the star there shot
> A rose-red sparkle to the city, and there
> Dwelt, and I knew it was the Holy Grail,
> Which never eyes on earth again shall see.

This is the ecstasy, the mysticism on which science and materialism have made their attack; and, noble as it is in Sir Galahad and in Percivale's sister—nobler far than the corruptions of social life which prevailed in King Arthur's court—it has too little of the reality of life to be of any permanent value to the human race.

But in striking contrast with these knights who pursue the Holy Grail is King Arthur himself with his purpose to build up a kingdom. He too has had a vision, but it is a vision "to make the world other" and to build up the realm of Christ. It is this purpose that binds him to the life about him, and causes him to see at once the folly of his knights when he learns of their vows. He realizes that for Galahad there may be such a vision. He will thus fulfill his nature, but the others will follow "wandering fires, lost in the quagmire." Men are they, and men's work they ought to do, with strength and will to right the wrongs of earth. What infinite pathos is in the king's words as he bids them farewell. His prophecy is fulfilled, as we have already seen, but what has been his work? He has tried with his few knights left to go

on in his efforts to organize a kingdom and help the suffering world. He is one of Carlyle's workmen, but is he no
more? Is he the practical man of whom we hear so much in
these days; has he no vision and faculty divine? Ambrosius
is the purely practical man, the other extreme from the
erring knights. He loves the world about him. How close
he is to mother earth and its frail humanity! He likes to
mingle with the folk in the little village, and knows every
honest face of theirs and every homely secret in their heart.
He delights himself with all their suffering and joys. He
lives

> like an old badger in his earth,
> With earth about him everywhere.

Now Arthur lives in a larger world than this. To the practical
love of humanity that characterizes Ambrosius he adds
something of the mystical sense of Galahad, and the two are
blended in an all but perfect manhood.

It is all summed up in the concluding paragraph, words
that need only to be read in the light of what has been said
to be instantly understood:

> And many a time they come,
> Until this earth he walks on seems not earth,
> This light that strikes his eyeball is not light,
> This air that smites his forehead is not air
> But vision—yea, his very hand and foot—
> In moments when he feels he cannot die,
> And knows himself no vision to himself,
> Nor the high God a vision, nor that One
> Who rose again.

These words were in Tennyson's mind the summing up of
all of Arthur's life, and his own. " 'The Holy Grail' is one

of the most imaginative of my poems," he once said; "I have expressed there my strong feeling as to the reality of the unseen. The end, when the king speaks of his work and of his visions, is intended to be the summing up of all in the highest note by the highest of human men. They are the central lines of the Idyls."

In other words, Tennyson did not find a dualism existing between the real and the ideal, the finite and the infinite, the temporal and the eternal, the human and the divine. His idealism, or his mysticism in the sense of the soul's union with God, is rooted in reality. He thus allies himself with the great mystics of all times. William Blake characterized such mysticism when he wrote his celebrated kuatrain:

> To see a world in a grain of sand,
> And a heaven in a wild flower;
> Hold infinity in the palm of your hand,
> And eternity in an hour.

CHAPTER V

DEFENDERS OF THE FAITH

THE subject of this chapter will recall the fact that Pope Leo hailed Henry VIII as the Defender of the Faith at a time when the English king was combating the ideas of Martin Luther. A later pope would have liked to recall the title when the king declared his independence of the Roman Church and despoiled and desecrated the cathedrals and monasteries. Be that as it may, there have always been defenders of the faith among English writers. Caedmon, writing from heavenly dictation his poetic accounts of Creation for a people recently in a state of barbarism; Piers the Plowman, at a time of religious corruption upholding the ideals and standards of Jesus; Edmund Spenser, combining the best elements of medieval faith with Platonic mysticism and the spirit of the Reformation; John Milton, fighting against oppression of every kind in the name of God and Christ, and fashioning under the worst possible conditions his epic of Puritanism; Dr. Johnson in the age of Voltaire stoutly defending a traditional faith—all these and many others who might be named have been defenders of the Christian faith.

In some of the previous chapters I have used religion in its broadest sense. Some of the men of whom I have written cannot be considered Christians. It is stretching the word to call Chaucer and Shakespeare Christians. Byron and Shelley would have repudiated the name. Many English writers would not have subscribed to some of the articles of faith insisted upon by many Christians. It is wise to use whatever they may have contributed to the interpretation of religion; for, as Hazlitt said, "A man may state many truths while coming to conclusions with which we do not agree." Such men are often the unconscious servants of the Most High.

The seventeenth century was especially an era when various beliefs and interpretations found expression. We have already considered Milton and Bunyan as exponents of the Puritan and Dissenting points of view. The newly established Anglican Church had as defenders Richard Hooker (*The Laws of Ecclesiastical Polity*), Sir Thomas Browne (*Religio Medici*), Jeremy Taylor (*Holy Living* and *Holy Dying*), and such poets as John Donne (*Sermons* and *Divine Poems*), George Herbert (*The Temple*), Henry Vaughan (*Sacred Poems*), and the recently discovered Thomas Traherne (*Centuries of Meditations* and *Poems*). In fact it was the golden age of Anglicanism; these divines and laymen magnified the Established Church as the true *via media* between Roman Catholicism and Puritanism, glorified the ritual and symbols, and gave a far fuller interpretation of Jesus as the central fact in Christianity than is generally recognized. The poems of Richard Crashaw showed that the Counter Reformation found a voice in England. If space allowed, it would be interesting to follow these crosscurrents of religious thought and feeling.

Most of the eighteenth-century writers were at least nominally Christians. Swift, savage as he was in his satire and cynicism, remained a clergyman and turned his strongest weapons on freethinkers and Dissenters. Pope's *Essay on*

Man may be considered from one angle as the poetic expression of Bolingbroke's philosophy, but Bishop Warburton was justified in claiming it as a Christian poem. It certainly crystallized the placid optimism and faith of the average eighteenth-century mind, or the twentieth-century for that matter. Addison was generally recognized as the outstanding Christian of his day, not only for having written his well-known hymn beginning "The spacious firmament on high," but because he tempered wit with morality and blended social charm and real piety. At the end of the century Dr. Johnson worshiped regularly at St. Clement's Danes in the Strand and wrote prayers that for deep religious feeling rival the hymns that voiced the Wesleyan revival. When he passed from the stage, Cowper, Blake, and Burns brought to English poetry a renaissance not only of beauty and feeling but of real religious emotion. The hymns of Cowper, the "Everlasting Gospel" and many shorter poems by Blake, "The Cotter's Saturday Night" and poems of repentance and longing by Burns—all helped prepare the way for the poets who have been considered in the preceding chapter, who did not realize all the religious values but who expressed as few men have the compelling presence of the Holy Spirit, and in the light of the Eternal and the Infinite revealed the beauty, wonder, and mystery of the universe and of the human soul.

II

With these brief suggestions of the valuable material to be found in other periods, I turn in this chapter to a special consideration of the literature of the Victorian period, for two reasons: I have devoted a lifetime to the study and interpretation of its writers, and religion was the prime concern of nearly all its leading men of letters.

Of this almost universal interest in religious questions I find a striking evidence in the Metaphysical Society, established in London in 1869. Among its members were the following: Dean Stanley, James Martineau, Cardinal Manning, and Frederick D. Maurice, as representatives of the clergy; of the scientists, Lubbock, Clifford, Tyndall, and Huxley; of the statesmen, Gladstone, John Morley, and Balfour; of the men of letters, Hutton, Bagehot, Froude, Frederick Harrison, Leslie Stephen, Ruskin, and Tennyson—the last named, strangely enough, being the originator of the idea of such a society. It was not technically a metaphysical society, for one of its members declared that after ten years of its existence no one had succeeded in defining the word "metaphysical"; but it was a body of men representing every variety of opinion seriously concerned about the spiritual problems of the age, and seeking for an answer to the mysteries of human life. What and whence am I? What is God? If a man die, shall he live again? What think ye of Christ? —these questions were answered sometimes in terms of science, sometimes in terms of philosophy, and again in terms of art. With few exceptions, all the commanding men of the Victorian era made contributions to what Matthew Arnold calls "the criticism of life."

It is natural that literature, whose chief characteristic is that it always gives the very form and pressure of the time that produces it, should in a very special sense be an interpretation of the spiritual life in its manifold aspects. As we have seen in Chapter III, the very industrialism of the age, with the superficial aspects of which Macaulay was so well satisfied, stirred Carlyle and Ruskin to a prophetic assertion of the moral rights of man. Nowhere outside of the prophets of the Old Testament will one find such denunciations of greed and luxury, or such a calling of men to the righteousness that exalteth a nation. Religion as elemental justice and as human sympathy is set forth in the burning language of *Fors Clavigera* and *Past* and *Present*. The Christian socialism of the time found expression in the novels of Kingsley and Charles Reade, and in a less direct but more appealing way in the humanitarian novels of Dickens and George Eliot. Democracy, imaginatively interpreted in the thrilling cosmic words of Walt Whitman, in the more formal verse of Lowell, and indirectly in the optimism and idealism of Emerson, was subjected to the severest criticism of English poets and men of letters, because it seemed to substitute the voice of the people for the voice of God.

Political interests, however, which had been dominant at the time of the French Revolution and well into the nineteenth century, became of less import than questions of faith. Science and the historical criticism of the Bible gave rise to "agnosticism," which was expressed now in the clear-cut, forceful words of Thomas Huxley and Herbert Spencer, now in the beautiful verses of Matthew Arnold and Edward FitzGerald, and in many a sad passage in the *Life and Letters* of George Eliot. The pathos of the spiritual unrest, the unsatisfied yearning of the human soul in the presence of doubts that would not clear, suggests "the ground tone of human agony." The conservatism of those who in the face of science and criticism sought refuge in the authority of tradition and dogma, or in the beauty of ceremony and art, as with the leaders of the Oxford Movement, reveals itself in the prose of Newman and in the poetry of John Keble. The great leaders of the Broad Church Movement, who sought to find a middle way out of the complexities of modern thought, who believed that emphasis should be laid not upon dogma or external authority but upon the essentials of the religious life, found in Tennyson and Browning the heralds of a new day of faith.

The most marked tendencies in literature, considered from a more artistic standpoint, were in the direction of an increasing emphasis on religion. The Romantic movement of the first part of the century had had three main characteristics: the reproduction of the life and spirit of the Middle Ages, a new feeling for nature, and an intense subjectivity that would be satisfied with nothing less than the infinite. These characteristics remained dominant, especially in the poetry of the new era. Medievalism, which in Scott had taken the form of the imaginative re-creation of the Age of Chivalry, in the Pre-Raphaelite Movement was manifest in a return to medieval art, which was essentially a religious art. While Rossetti and his colleagues were in some respects abnormal in their lives and in their ideals, and while Ruskin was eccentric in his judgments of paintings and buildings, the real significance of the movement was well suggested by Browning in his "Old Pictures in Florence." The prime object of the painters before Raphael and of their disciples in England was

> To bring the invisible full into play!
> Let the visible go to the dogs—what matters?

It is a striking fact that the origins of this looking back to the art and architecture of the Middle Ages must be found in the Oxford Movement, which sought to restore the medieval church.

It is also true that many of the Victorian writers were

drawn by an irresistible current into the artistic representation of religious questions. Carlyle was at first an interpreter of German literature and a critic of English; but he became an original force in England only when he gave to the world his spiritual autobiography, *Sartor Resartus,* four chapters of which, the "Centre of Indifference," the "Sorrows of Teufelsdröckh," "The Everlasting No," and "The Everlasting Yea," represent not only his own spiritual travail and triumph, but that of his age as well. There were among the poets few "idle singers of an empty day" like Morris, or pagan hedonists reveling in the sensuousness of language like Swinburne. Matthew Arnold, in the preface to his first volume of poems, laid down the general law that art should be impersonal, and cited the Greeks to uphold him. His first poems were lacking in substance; in his later poetry he became more and more concerned about "the strange disease," "the sick fatigue" of modern thought, "the hopeless tangle of the age." Tennyson's first poems were mere exercises in verse—"lollipops," Carlyle called them—but after the death of Arthur Hallam he passed through a struggle with doubt and despair that issued in the triumphant faith of "Ulysses," "The Two Voices," and *In Memoriam.* Browning alone of all the writers was from the first dominated by the master passion of religion. In *Paracelsus,* written when he was twenty-two, he came to his full maturity as a thinker, the last two hundred lines of the poem still remaining perhaps his most important summing up of life and the universe.

III

While it is exceedingly difficult to summarize in one chapter the religious life and thought of a complex age like the one under consideration, it is well, I think, to suggest some of its most marked tendencies and thus to try to make some sort of synthesis. It may be possible to find a Pilgrim's Progress of the past century—a progress from faith through doubt and unrest back to a larger faith. An additional interest attaches to such a study in that religious thought still centers about the same issues. One may easily find parallels between types of the Victorian era and those of today. The various individuals show dispositions, temperaments, attitudes of mind, that are more or less typical of human nature in any age. The radical, the conservative, the liberal—the last occupying a sort of middle ground between the other two—these we have always, and some of the characteristics of each type are writ large in the literature of the Victorian era.

Many forces conspired to unsettle the faith of men in God and immortality. First among these should be mentioned the general cataclysm caused by the French Revolution, for its effect on religion was world wide. The feeling of weariness and of despair so powerfully expressed by Byron remained as an inheritance of later writers—Arnold, for instance:

> Down came the storm! O'er France it passed
> In sheets of scathing fire.
>
> . . . . . .
>
> Down came the storm! In ruins fell
> The worn-out world we knew.

This was a Victorian echo of Byron's melancholy musings over the ruins of the past. English philosophical radicalism was a logical descendant of some of the ideas of the Encyclopedists, and in part of the utilitarianism of Bentham and Mill. Positivism, with its matter-of-fact ethics and its well-articulated system of thought, was a foe to spiritual insight.

Of more moment was the new historical criticism that originated in Germany. From the discussion of the Homeric poems German scholars passed to the consideration of the early Church, the historical setting of Paul and the real meaning of his epistles, and then the Gospels—applying to all the tests of critical scholarship. The effect of all this on literature may be seen in the fact that George Eliot, in translating Strauss's *Das Leben Jesu,* so fell under its influence that she gave up the faith of her early life—she grew "ill with dissecting the beautiful story of the Crucifixion." Matthew Arnold, like the great French writer Renan, adopted many of the methods and ideas of the new criticism; in *Literature and Dogma, St. Paul and Protestantism,* and other books, he did much to popularize the intelligent study of the Bible and at the same time to shake the faith of those who had before accepted the orthodox view of the Scriptures.

The criticism of the Bible was strengthened by the revelations of science, and the opposition to the Christian point of view by the scientific method and spirit. In view of the tremendous achievements of science in the conquest of the material world and in the alleviation of human suffering, as well as in its contribution to almost every field of knowledge, it is small wonder that men turned to its leaders as offering new solutions to the problem of human life. A reading of the lives of Darwin and Huxley and of the writings of Tyndall and Spencer is almost necessary to one who would understand the literature or the religious thought of the period. Huxley says that, when he began his scientific career, he saw posted up all over the physical universe: "No thoroughfare. By order. Moses." In other words, Genesis and science were in conflict. With the instincts of a born fighter he waged war upon a religion that set up the Scriptures as

153

the final authority on everything. He agreed with some of his adversaries in saying that Christian theology must stand or fall on the basis of the historical accuracy of the Jewish Scriptures.

Men of our time, and indeed many of his contemporaries, have found other ways of stating the controversy, but in the midst of the fight the whole weight of science seemed to be thrown against religion. Physiological psychology, combined with the results of biological research, seemed to strike at faith in immortality, the magic word "evolution" to do away with the necessity for a God, and materialism to supplant any theory of the supernatural. Darwin, with characteristic modesty and candor, published his results without giving them a philosophical interpretation; but Huxley, one of the best debaters and writers of his day, used every weapon of reason, ridicule, and persuasion to popularize and make prevail the scientific method and conclusions. Herbert Spencer, taking all knowledge to be his province, elaborated an entire system of thought, the basis of which was his theory of the "Unknowable."

IV

The opposition to Christianity, which had in previous ages taken the form of atheism, or deism, or gnosticism, in the Victorian period took the form of "agnosticism." Huxley has given a highly interesting account of his finding a name for himself in the Metaphysical Society, previously referred to. He was the only man without the rag of a label to cover himself with, the only fox without a tail:

When I reached intellectual maturity and began to ask myself whether I was an atheist, a theist, or a pantheist; a materialist or an idealist; a Christian or a freethinker; I found that the more I learned and reflected, the less ready was the answer; until, at last, I came to the conclusion that I had neither art nor part with any of these denominations, except the last. The one thing in which most of these people were agreed was the one thing in which I differed from them. They were quite sure they had attained a certain "gnosis"—had, more or less successfully, solved the problem of existence; while I was quite sure I had not, and had a pretty strong conviction that the problem was insoluable. . . .

So I took thought, and invented what I conceived to be the appropriate title of "agnostic." . . . I, too, had a tail like the other foxes.

And that is likewise Darwin's conclusion of the whole matter: "I cannot pretend to throw the least light on the whole abstruse problem. The mystery of the beginning of all things is insoluble, and I for one must be content to remain an agnostic." To a German student he wrote, "The safest conclusion seems to me that the whole subject is beyond the reach of man's intellect, but man can do his duty." Tyndall, who had something more of imagination and of the poetical in him than either Huxley or Darwin, said that he had as little fellowship with the atheist who says there is no God, as with the theist who professes to know the mind of God. "But if the Materialist is confounded and Science rendered dumb, who else is prepared with a solution? To whom has the Word of the Lord been revealed? Let us bow our heads, and acknowledge our ignorance, priest and philosopher, one and all."

There is a certain satisfaction, a certain peace, as these "masters of the modern mind" dismiss the mysteries of life and settle down to the contemplation of the seen and the known—a satisfaction broken only now and then by a sigh such as Huxley's letter about his dead wife, or Tyndall's yearning like a pilgrim for his distant home, or Darwin's almost pathetic confession of the loss of his interest in religion and art. Those who were greatly influenced by science or historical criticism, who partook of the spirit of the age, and yet *felt* as well as thought, and studied and sympathized with men as well as with nature, did not rest so calmly in agnosticism. Mr. Gates, in an illuminating essay on Arnold, says in contrasting him with men of science: "Yet Arnold has a far wider range of sensibilities than any one of them; life plays upon him in far richer and more various ways; it touches him into response through associations that have a more distinctively human character, and that have a deeper and warmer color of emotion drawn out of the past of the race." There is still, with all of George Eliot's passion for science, and all of Arnold's gospel of criticism, and all of Edward FitzGerald's epicureanism, some of the romantic yearning for faith. One feels that in Arnold's prose there is not always the high seriousness which he himself put down as one of the necessary qualities of great poetry, but in his poetry we are always in the presence of a sincere and earnest questioning and nearly always of a melancholy that is incurable. There is to me nothing more touching in modern poetry than Arnold's yearning for a faith that could never be his. Sometimes, as for instance when he speaks of his father in "Rugby Chapel," or thinks of the pursuit of the ideal symbolized in the "Scholar-Gypsy"and Clough, he attains a certain minimum of faith; but in the main his poetry is a poetry of doubt, haunting in its melancholy. This sadness is like the eternal note of sadness in the sea:

Sophocles long ago
Heard it on the Ægean, and it brought
Into his mind the turbid ebb and flow
Of human misery; we
Find also in the sound a thought,
Hearing it by this distant northern sea.

The sea of faith,
Was once, too, at the full, and round earth's shore
Lay like the folds of a bright girdle furl'd.
But now I only hear
Its melancholy, long, withdrawing roar,
Retreating, to the breath
Of the night-wind, down the vast edges drear
And naked shingles of the world.

Unable to accept the old faith and unwilling to accept any
substitute, he represents the modern man as

Wandering between two worlds, one dead,
The other powerless to be born,
With nowhere yet to rest my head,
Like these, on earth I wait forlorn.
Their faith, my tears, the world deride:
I come to shed them at their side.

.   .   .   .   .

For the world cries, your faith is now
But a dead time's exploded dream;
My melancholy, sciolists say,
Is a pass'd mode, an outworn theme,—
As if the world had ever had
A faith, or sciolists been sad!

Ah! if it *be* pass'd, take away,
At least, the restlessness, the pain!

> Be man henceforth no more a prey
> To these out-dated stings again!
> The nobleness of grief is gone;
> Ah, leave us not the fret alone!

V

There have been many ways of escape from the unrest that sounds in these lines and in many another passage of Victorian prose and poetry. One may be utterly impatient with such doubt, or he may be indifferent. He may, as Arnold said of Wordsworth, "put by the cloud of mortal destiny" or "avert his ken from half of human fate," finding complete peace in nature. He may, like Sénancour, flee from the sick fatigue of modern thought to the Alps. To others, science offers a sure way out of the perplexities by frankly adopting a complacent agnosticism.

Arnold in his poem "Stanzas from the Grande Chartreuse" suggests another way of escape—that of retreat to the past. The silent courts, the cowled forms in gleaming white, the austere beauty of the chapel, the library, the garden of "the Carthusians' world-famed home"—all suggest the medieval church in contrast with the hurry and perplexity of modern life. Forgetting for a moment the teaching of the masters of the modern mind, he cries:

> Oh, hide me in your gloom profound,
> Ye solemn seats of holy pain!
> Take me, cowled forms, and fence me round,
> Till I possess my soul again!

He might have had in mind, in writing these lines, the leaders of the Oxford Movement, and especially John Henry Newman. To some Newman is merely a Catholic who showed a remarkable lack of intellectual vigor; but the movement which he led for twelve years within the Church of England represents such a marked tendency in human nature and in the particular period that it deserves more than passing notice.

His autobiography, *Apologia pro vita sua*, written as a reply to the uncharitable attack of Charles Kingsley, is one of the most interesting of human documents. At fifteen, he tells us, he fell under the influence of a definite creed and received into his intellect "impressions of dogma which, through God's mercy, have never been effaced or obscured." "A few months later, I drew up a series of texts in support of each verse of the Athanasian Creed." Tradition had its hold upon him. "If we would learn doctrine, we must have access to the formularies of the Church; for instance, to the Catechism and the creeds." At Oxford, as a student, he was for a time "tainted" with the liberalism of Dr. Thomas Arnold's pupils, whom he soon after regarded as "an intellectual circle afflicted with the pride of reason." He speaks of liberalism as "the mistake of subjecting to human judgment those revealed doctrines which are in their nature beyond and independent of it, and of claiming to determine on intrinsic grounds the truth and value of propositions which rest for their reception on the external authority of the Divine Word." Along with conscience he puts the Bible, the church, and antiquity as authorities of equal weight. "Ten thousand difficulties do not make a doubt," he says, and adds that he never had a doubt!

He found fellowship with John Keble and Hurrell Froude, both of them connected, like Newman, with Oriel College, Oxford. In 1833, Froude and Newman went to the Continent, but all the time they were thinking and talking of the work to be done at home. The sense of a divine mission to withstand the increasing liberalism of the time took hold of them. Much as Newman loved the beauty and the ruins of Europe, the voice of duty called him, as it called Milton two centuries before; neither of them could selfishly pursue his own culture or pleasure while a conflict was waging in England between what each conceived to be the powers of light and darkness. At last Newman put off in an orange boat, bound for Marseilles, and on a memorable night wrote the most beautiful of modern hymns, "Lead, Kindly Light,"—it was a prayer for the light to guide him in the coming darkness.

The Sunday after he landed, July 14, 1833, Keble, who had been for several years attempting to spiritualize the forms and ritual of the Church of England, preached at Oxford the Assize Sermon, which is generally considered the beginning of the Oxford Movement. A few days later there was held a meeting of Oxford and Cambridge men who were concerned about the state of the church, "assailed by enemies from without and within." It was the time of the Reform Bill, when the very existence of the church seemed threatened. One of the men, Rose, had studied in Germany, and could therefore give a first-hand account of the battle waging there between orthodoxy and heresy. The great masses of the English clergy were indifferent, almost as deficient in spiritual fervor as the preachers of the eighteenth century. These enthusiastic young men determined to sound the bugle for an advance against the enemies of the established faith. "I wished," says Newman, "to make a strong pull with all who were opposed to the principles of liberalism, whoever they might be." The supreme question was, How to keep the church from being liberalized? Rather than have the liberal view prevail, he says, "I do not shrink from uttering my conviction that it would be a gain to the world were it vastly more superstitious, more bigoted, more gloomy, more fierce in its religion, than it now shows itself to be."

Of the several expedients planned to carry on the crusade—the organization of associations throughout the country, a public address to the Archbishop of Canterbury, and the publication of tracts—the last was to cause the greatest effect, and the movement was sometimes known as the Tractarian Movement. These tracts were "like the short, sharp, rapid utterances of men in pain and danger and pressing emergency." The first one, published September 9, 1833, closed with the significant words: "At all events choose your side. To remain neuter much longer will be itself to take sides. 'He that is not with Me is against Me.' "

But the greatest influence in winning public attention and following was Newman himself as he preached in St. Mary's Church. Oxford, "whispering from her towers the last enchantments of the Middle Age," appealed to him as the fit background for a great religious awakening. There are few greater passages in modern prose than that in which Matthew Arnold speaks of the voices that came to him while he was a student at Oxford:

No such voices as those which we heard in our youth at Oxford are sounding there now. Oxford has more criticism now, more knowledge, more light; but such voices as those of our youth it has no longer. The name of Cardinal Newman is a great name to the imagination still; his genius and style are still things of power. . . . Forty years ago he was in the very prime of life; he was close at hand to us at Oxford; he was preaching in St. Mary's pulpit every Sunday; he seemed about to transform and renew what was for us the most national and natural institution in the world, the Church of England. Who could resist the charm of that spiritual apparition, gliding in the dim afternoon light through the aisles of St. Mary's, rising into the pulpit, and then, in the most entrancing of voices, breaking the silence with words and thoughts which were a religious music—subtle, sweet, mournful? I seem to hear him still, saying: "After the fever of life, . . . at length comes death, at length the white throne of God, at length the beatific vision."

This is Newman at his best. Those of us who never saw or heard him, never came under the spell of his personality, get much of the same effect in his best writings. The clearness, the melody, the rich imaginativeness of his prose style are known of all men. He was really a poet of the mystic imagination.

And yet alongside of the picture that Arnold draws of Newman at the height of his power and influence, I always place that other passage of another Oxford man, John Campbell Shairp, who tells of the effect Newman's going to the Roman Church had on the men of the university who had followed him with such confidence. It was like the muffling, if not the silencing, of a magic voice:

How vividly comes back the remembrance of the aching blank, the awful pause, which fell on Oxford when that voice had ceased, and we knew that we should hear it no more! It was as when one kneeling in the night, in the silence of some vast cathedral, the great bell tolling solemnly overhead has suddenly gone still. Some then began to look this way and that for new teachers, and to rush vehemently to the opposite extremes of thought. But there were those who could not so lightly forget. On Sunday forenoons and evenings in the retirement of their rooms, the printed words of those marvelous sermons would thrill them till they wept abundant and most sweet tears. Since then many voices of powerful teachers they may have heard, but none that ever penetrated the soul like his.

That Newman was honest in becoming a Catholic nobody can doubt. His temperament, his logical mind, his strong sense of tradition, his sensitiveness to the aesthetic charm of the Catholic ritual—all led him to the Mother Church. There was for him no halfway house between atheism and Catholicism.

One sees the conservative at his best in men like Newman and Sir Walter Scott and Edmund Burke—men who throw around the past the glamour of their reverence, their imagination, and their love. Here we have tradition touched with sentiment; and the charm is perhaps all the greater when the struggle they make against new ideas is a futile one—when they fight against the stars in their courses. The conservative is scarcely so admirable when he adopts ridicule as his weapon of attack. A case in point is the speech that Bishop Wilberforce, a High-churchman who did not follow Newman into the Catholic Church, made at the meeting of the British Scientific Association in the midst of the controversy about evolution. Turning to Huxley, who was seated upon the platform, he asked whether the scientist was related by his grandmother or his grandfather to an ape. Huxley, in reply, rebuked him in words that inevitably strike one as just:

I asserted, and I repeat, that a man has no reason to be ashamed of having an ape for a grandfather. If there were an ancestor whom I should feel shame in recalling, it would be a man, a man of restless and versatile intellect, who, not content with an equivocal success in his own sphere of life, plunges into scientific questions with which he has no real acquaintance, only to obscure them by an aimless rhetoric and distract the attention of hearers from the real point at issue by eloquent digressions and skilled appeals to religious prejudice.

The religious conservative appears to even worse advantage when he uses the power of an ecclesiastical system, or the tyranny of an unintelligent public opinion, to stifle free thought. Newman had iron in his frame and gall in his blood when he said of certain Anglican divines: "I was in a humor to bite off their ears." Whether the organization be the Catholic Church crushing the Modernist Movement, or the Church of England persecuting the Oxford and Broad Church movements, or the more evangelical churches putting the emphasis upon doctrinal standards rather than upon vital religion, all alike seem to deny the continual revelation of truth through successive ages. They would set a limit to the revelation of the Spirit of God, and would persecute the seekers after Truth.

VI

The opposition of the Oxford Movement to liberalism in religion and to all the conclusions of modern thought did not satisfy many of the most devout men of the age. Hence arose the Broad Church Movement, which had its origin in the conversations of Coleridge at Highgate, when he sought to inspire younger men like John Sterling with the idea that German transcendentalism offered a better interpretation of the Christian religion than was found in the apologetics of the eighteenth century. The pupils of Dr. Thomas Arnold of Rugby, of whose liberalism Newman complained, imbibed the breadth of the great headmaster's spirit. Dean Stanley, Frederick D. Maurice, Frederick W. Robertson, and the authors of the *Essays and Reviews,* differing as they did in details of thought and faith, were all characterized by a certain reasonableness, a tolerance of spirit, a desire to mediate between the old faith and the new revelations of science, philosophy, and scholarship—and some of them by an evangelical fervor. Carlyle maintained that Stanley was boring holes in the Church of England; but he was really stopping up the holes, fitting the ship for a perilous journey ahead of her by overhauling the rigging and by making use of improved methods of navigation.

The writings of none of these men attained to such literary quality as we have in Newman, but they had as allies the two greatest poets of the Victorian era. Not that Tennyson and Browning were theologians, but their attitude to the religious problems of the age was similar to that of the leaders of the Broad Church Movement. Robertson wrote one of the best commentaries on *In Memoriam.* Maurice in dedicating his *Theological Essays* to Tennyson, who had for years been one of his best friends, said:

I have maintained in *Essays* that a theology that does not correspond to the deepest thoughts and feelings of human beings cannot be a true theology. Your writings have taught men to enter into these thoughts and feelings. There are some who long that the bells of our churches may indeed

> "Ring out the darkness of the land,
> Ring in the Christ that is to be."

Gladstone hit the mark when he said that Tennyson had done much "to harmonize the new draught of external power with the old and more mellowing faith, self-devotion, loyalty, reverence, and discipline." Not in terms of theology, but of life, he was the mediator between the new thought and the old faith. But he attained to this distinction only after the most acute struggle and almost overwhelming doubt. What he said of Hallam applies exactly to himself:

> One indeed I knew
> In many a subtle question versed,
> Who touch'd a jarring lyre at first,
> But ever strove to make it true:
>
> Perplext in faith, but pure in deeds,
> At last he beat his music out.
> There lives more faith in honest doubt,
> Believe me, than in half the creeds.
>
> He fought his doubts and gather'd strength,
> He would not make his judgment blind,
> He faced the spectres of the mind
> And laid them: thus he came at length
>
> To find a stronger faith his own.

He would not evade the questions suggested by science. He was so thorough a student of science as to win the approbation of even Huxley. Science afforded him many exact similes and metaphors; but, more than that, it transformed many of his ideas of nature and man. In "By an Evolutionist," he accepts the animal origin of man's body; but the soul holds the scepter; it comes from God and returns to him.

Huxley might say: "Compare the brightly-colored lichen and the painter to whom it is instinct with beauty, or the botanist whom it feeds with knowledge. And yet they are all the same." And Tyndall: "All our philosophy, all our poetry, all our science, and all our arts, Plato, Shakespeare, Newton and Raphael, are potential in the fires of the sun." And yet, in the face of these seeming teachings of science, Tennyson exclaims:

> I trust I have not wasted breath:
> > I think we are not wholly brain,
> > Magnetic mockeries; not in vain,
> Like Paul with beasts, I fought with Death;
>
> Not only cunning casts in clay:
> > Let Science prove we are, and then
> > What matters Science unto men,
> At least to me? I would not stay.
>
> Let him, the wiser man who springs
> > Hereafter, up from childhood shape
> > His action like the greater ape,
> But I was *born* to other things.

If nature, "red in tooth and claw," brings destruction to individuals and types, and suggests the passing of man into the void, the poet yet appeals to the God of love as creator of the moral law. This God can be found only by the heart and imagination of man:

> That which we dare invoke to bless;
> > Our dearest faith; our ghastliest doubt;
> > He, They, One, All; within, without;
> The Power in darkness whom we guess;
>
> I found Him not in world or sun,
> > Or eagle's wing, or insect's eye;
> > Nor thro' the questions men may try,
> The petty cobwebs we have spun:
>
> If e'er when faith had fall'n asleep,
> > I heard a voice "believe no more"

167

And heard an ever-breaking shore
That tumbled in the Godless deep;

A warmth within the breast would melt
The freezing reason's colder part,
And like a man in wrath the heart
Stood up and answer'd "I have felt."

No, like a child in doubt and fear:
But that blind clamor made me wise;
Then was I as a child that cries,
But, crying, knows his father near;

And what I am beheld again
What is, and no man understands;
And out of darkness came the hands
That reach thro' nature, moulding men.

VII

Among all the voices that come to us from the Victorian era, some of them urging a retreat to the chivalry and art and faith of the Middle Ages, some finding in the calm and serenity of nature the balm of Gilead, some completely satisfied with the attitude of science or with the indifference or irreverence of critical scholarship, others with "no language but a cry" under the darkened heavens, and still others somewhat feeble after a hard-fought contest with doubt—among all these there rings out, clear and strong, the great voice of Robert Browning. For a long time neglected and ridiculed, he now appears to a constantly increasing number of men and women as the most buoyant, the most virile, and the most inspiring poet of the nineteenth century. Some are drawn to him by reason of his dramatic art in those poems where he transcends the limitations that mar more than half his poetry. Some appreciate most keenly his proclamation of the wild joys of living—the glory of abounding physical life. Others, travelers and students of art and lovers of music, realize that no other poet can be so often quoted in the art galleries of Europe or in the music halls of Boston and New York. To some he is the best love poet we have, in that he has drawn love from every possible standpoint and reached a climax in expressing the greatest love story of the century. But most people feel, I think, that while all these points of view are important, he is pre-eminently "the friend and aider of those who would live in the spirit." In an age where there were so much indifference, doubt, and pessimism, he was, as Chesterton has well said, "something far more convincing, far more comforting, far more religiously significant than an optimist; he was a happy man." In his poetry all the discords of his age are harmonized. In this novel, quick, variegated world, he was "aware of a central peace where the noise was quieted and the tangle unraveled."

What makes Browning's faith so significant is that he approached the whole question, not from the standpoint of reason alone, but from that of human life. No other English writer since Shakespeare has created such a variety of characters or manifests such a range of observation of life. He had something of the myriad-mindedness that Coleridge found in Shakespeare. He was a dramatist, not in his mastery of theatrical art nor in the use of dialogue, but in his mastery of his own art form, the dramatic monologue, which in his hands became the means of revealing the inner life and thought of a great variety of men and women of every conceivable type, from all the countries of Europe, from almost every period of the world's history—thought in all its subtlest forms, passion in all its varied phases from the most earthly to the most divine, the will now failing to follow the behests of the spirit, now triumphing over defeat and misfortune and tragedy, and charging like the fighters of old through the mists of death.

His faith was not due to the suppression of anything, but to the transcending of all obstacles and difficulties. He was alive at every point of his being. He had a marvelous intellect; the difficulty with his poetry is that his active intellectual power was not always fused with imagination and emotion. But he knew that "admiration, hope, love—these make mankind." He was aware of the conclusions of critical scholarship—witness "A Death in the Desert," "Christmas-Eve," and the speech of Renan in the Epilogue to *Dramatis Personae*. In many poems he shows his knowledge of Greek art and literature—witness "Cleon" and *Balaustion's Adventure*—but he was not a Hellenist like Arnold or Pater; for he knew that what Euripides guessed at Paul knew, and that what Cleon, the representative of all that was best in Greek culture, needed was the gospel the "mere barbarian Jew" was then preaching on Mars Hill. He knew even better than Ruskin or Rossetti the art of Italy—witness "Andrea del Sarto" and "Fra Lippo Lippi"—but he was no aesthete; his characters are full-blooded men and women rather than the pale figures of Rossetti's canvas. He appreciated the faith of the Middle Ages—witness the Pope in *The Ring and the Book*—but unlike Newman he portrayed the darker side of Catholicism in "Soliloquy of the Spanish Cloister" and "The Confessional." Although he did not know science as well as Tennyson, he divined its doctrine of evolution—witness the concluding lines of *Paracelsus* and "Francis Furini"—but he knew that, while science could reveal many facts and processes, it could never discover the underlying power and love of the universe. He had much of that individual unrest under the restrictions and limitations of life that writers from Blake to Bernard Shaw have voiced; but he balanced this individualism with the enduring ideals of discipline, loyalty, and faith.

Moncure D. Conway tells us that it was often a matter of wonder among his rationalistic friends how Browning, with all this knowledge and this versatility of thought, could be a Christian. I have mentioned in Chapter I that the poet James Thomson, himself an unbeliever, suggested a paper for someone in the future to write, "How Can Browning Be a Christian?" Browning has himself answered that question, not only in his poems, but in some letters that leave no doubt of his faith in the Christian religion. He says, speaking of Christianity:

I know all that may be said against it on the ground of history, of reason, or even moral sense. But I am not the less convinced that the life and death of Christ, as Christians apprehend them, supply something which humanity requires, and that it is true for them.

And again:

The evidence of divine power is everywhere about us; not so the evidence of divine love. That love could only reveal itself to the human heart by some supreme act of human tenderness and devotion: the fact or fancy of Christ's cross or passion could alone supply such a revelation.

In the same year that *In Memoriam* appeared—in the middle of the century, when, as Froude says in his *Life of Carlyle,* "the compasses were all awry, the lights all drifting, and nothing left to steer by except the stars"—there was published Browning's *Christmas-Eve and Easter-Day*, an even stronger, though less popular, poem than the former. There is an even more buoyant faith in immortality, a more vigorous assertion of the conflict of life from the religious point of view, and, what is more significant, a setting forth of the need of the human heart for the revelation that came to the world when the Word was made flesh. In spite of the analysis by the German scholar of the "myth of Christ"— "the exhausted air-bell of the critic"—in spite of the pomp and circumstance of religion as seen in a service at St. Peter's, in spite of the narrowness and poverty of spirit as seen in the little evangelical chapel, Browning presents us a radiant image of Christ as he appeared to him transfigured by the moonlight. In this poem, as in so many others, he shows himself aware of all the tendencies of modern thought, and at the same time expresses his belief that the only solution of man's problems lies in the Incarnation—not set forth in a theological formula with the emphasis on the commercial and legal statement of the Atonement, but Christ as the Way, the Truth, the Life.

"A Death in the Desert"—with its dramatic representation of the dying beloved disciple—was written soon after Strauss's *Das Leben Jesu* appeared, and as a direct answer to it. The keynote is in the lines:

> I say, the acknowledgment of God in Christ
> Accepted by thy reason, solves for thee
> All questions in the earth and out of it.

The incompleteness of the idea of Jehovah and of the religion of the Jews is brought out with great dramatic power in the book of Job, in which the suffering patriarch, throwing away the old conception of God that the theologians of his day presented, reaches out after the hope of immortality and of a "daysman," or mediator, who might reveal the ways of the Almighty to man. The same problem Browning has presented in "Saul," a poem in which Browning is as supreme in his mastery of poetic art as he is in his vision of life. The poem is all-inclusive—a good summary of all the powers that enter into true culture and true religion. The beauty of nature, the wild joys of living, the inspiring idea of immortality in the race, are all expressed in memorable poetry. These all lead up to the climax of the poem—the prophecy of the supreme revelation in Christ:

Would I suffer for him that I love? So wouldst thou—so wilt
    thou! . . .
As thy Love is discovered almighty, almighty be proved
Thy power, that exists with and for it, of being Beloved!
He who did most, shall bear most; the strongest shall stand
    the most weak.
'Tis the weakness in strength, that I cry for! my flesh, that I
    seek
In the Godhead! I seek and I find it. O Saul, it shall be
A Face like my face that receives thee; a Man like to me,
Thou shalt love and be loved by, forever: a Hand like this hand
Shall throw open the gates of new life to thee! See the Christ
    stand!

Browning deals further with the central truth of the Incarnation in "An Epistle of Karshish," in "Cleon," and later in *The Ring and the Book*. If it be urged that those are merely dramatic poems, and that we cannot take them as expressing the poet's own faith, we should refer to the Epilogue to *Dramatis Personae*. There is always special significance in

Browning's epilogues; in them he speaks *in propria persona* of art and life. In this epilogue he represents David as speaking in behalf of Israel, when people gathered only at stated times in the temple to rejoice in the worship of God. The second speaker is Renan, who tells of the loss of faith in Christ in recent times. As he looks up into the heavens he finds the star of Bethlehem "all gone across the dark so far"—"lost in the night at last." Men are left with only the lesser lights; they can no longer look up and know they themselves are seen, speak and be sure they are heard. Then Browning speaks, saying that there is no longer any need of a temple, for "the walls o' the world are that"; all men can join in the worship of God. The star of Bethlehem is not gone:

> That one Face, far from vanish, rather grows,
> Or decomposes but to recompose,
> Become my universe that feels and knows!

Mrs. Sutherland Orr, the biographer of Browning, tells us that the poet said to her one day, as he finished reading this poem to her: "That's the way I feel Christ." With this beautiful figure of the Face of Christ lighting up the universe, we may leave the consideration of the Victorian Age.

VIII

One reason I have stressed the Victorian period is that so many of the problems that then faced men are still dominant in our own age. Science has gone on from strength to strength advancing and making claims for its authority in every field of human life and thought. It has not only won *a* place in the sun but *the* place. In biology, psychology, sociology, and philosophy the effects wrought out in the preceding era have gone far beyond the claims of Huxley or the revelations of Darwin. Bertrand Russell's *A Free Man's Worship* and various treatises on behaviorism, as well as a great many novels and plays and even poems, have dominated the thought of many men in this generation.

At the same time there has been a remarkable development in both England and America of Roman Catholicism. I refer not only to the increasing membership, the church buildings, and ecclesiastical organization, but to the poetry of Francis Thompson and Gerard Manly Hopkins, who were influenced respectively by Cardinal Manning and Cardinal Newman. In the home of the Meynells in London some of the most brilliant young men in England found both aesthetic enjoyment and religious conviction. Over against George Bernard Shaw, who is the embodiment of so many of the main tendencies of modern thought, stood an equally brilliant personality and master of epigrammatic style— Gilbert Chesterton, an ardent convert to Catholicism. It is not strange that Willa Cather, probably the greatest of American contemporary novelists, should have written *Death Comes for the Archbishop* and soon thereafter found her way to the Catholic Church. The large number of Newman groups in our colleges is evidence that the voice of Newman still sounds.

Nor is the Victorian compromise between these two extremes without a successor. Masefield's *The Everlasting Mercy,* Vachel Lindsay's "General Booth" and "I Hear Immanuel Singing," and, even more notably, T. S. Eliot's poems and prose writings point the way out of the "Waste Land," which he so piquantly revealed as the result of much modern thought, to the cathedral and the Rock. No modern writer has been more sensitive to all the currents of modern thought than H. G. Wells. He has repeatedly prophesied "things to come." I know of no better conclusion to this volume than the conclusion of his *Outline of History,* which the reader may interpret as going far beyond Wells's own questionable faith:

Out of the trouble and tragedy of this present time there may emerge a moral and intellectual revival, a religious revival, of a simplicity and scope to draw together men of alien races and now discrete traditions into one common and sustained way of living for the world's service. . . . The beginnings of such things are never conspicuous. Great movements of the racial soul come at first "like a thief in the night," and then suddenly are discovered to be powerful and world-wide. Religious emotion—stripped of corruptions and freed from its last priestly entanglements—may presently blow through life again like a great wind, bursting the doors and flinging open the shutters of the individual life, and making many things possible and easy that in these present days of exhaustion seem almost too difficult to desire. . . . There is a social consciousness at work in our minds and hearts that will yet deliver as from the wicked man. In spite of much occasion for pessimism to-day, there is occasion for greater optimism than man ever before had.[1]

We may look forward with confidence to a renaissance of literature and a revival of religion. What happened at the end of the eighteenth century may well happen in the immediate future—the renewal of the human spirit after an age of prose and reason, of skepticism and materialism. We may say with Matthew Arnold that the future of poetry is immense.

[1] By permission of the publisher, Doubleday, Doran & Co.

DATE DUE

Curtis			
Kathryn			
Eng Sem			
(B) P.C			
APR 21 1986			
APR 18 1988			
APR 09 1994			
GAYLORD			PRINTED IN U.S A.

The Author

EDWIN MIMS was for thirty years head of the English department of Vanderbilt University, as well as chairman of the humanities division, until his retirement in 1942. Now as a professor emeritus he is in constant demand as a lecturer in all parts of the country. He conducts a correspondence course and teaches in pastors' schools for the Methodist Commission on Ministerial Training, is a special lecturer in various colleges for the Phi Beta Kappa Society, and speaks before summer assemblies and institutes.

When Vanderbilt was still young, Dr. Mims entered as a student from his native Arkansas and stayed for his B.A. (1892) and M.A. (1893) degrees as well as a year as instructor. During the next fifteen years he was professor of English at Trinity College, now Duke University, meanwhile completing work for his Ph.D. (1900) degree at Cornell University. After three years teaching at the University of North Carolina he was called back to his alma mater in 1912.

The spiritual influence of Dr. Mims' career as a teacher can be rivaled only by the greatest ministers. Thousands of gray-headed Vanderbilt alumni can quote at the drop of a hat the thrilling conclusion of Tennyson's "Ulysses" with its call to "seek a newer world"—his invariable first assignment in the course required of all freshman. To students through the years he opened up a new world not only of beauty in literature but even more of "elevated thoughts" on the greatest values of life. For, lover of beauty of phase though he is, he has never been satisfied to analyze style and diction or yet to pry into sources and "influences" but rather has sought in the work of each writer the noblest expressions of the heights of the human spirit.

Dr. Mims is author of biographies of Sidney Lanier and Chancellor James H. Kirkland, *The Advancing South*, and *Adventurous America;* and editor of anthologies and textbook editions of classics. His writings have appeared in many periodicals as well as in encyclopedias and the like. But in *GREAT WRITERS AS INTERPRETERS OF RELIGION* his students will recognize that he has summed up as never elsewhere the greatest spiritual messages he has discovered in a lifetime of interpreting the best in English and American literature.